Mill Street, Dorchester

Thomas Hardy's Mixen Lane

Mill Street, Dorchester

Thomas Hardy's Mixen Lane

David J. Forrester

Roving Press

Published by Roving Press Ltd
4 Southover Cottages, Frampton, Dorset, DT2 9NQ, UK
Tel: +44 (0)1300 321531, www.rovingpress.co.uk

First published 2016 by Roving Press Ltd

ISBN: 978-1-906651-305

British Library Cataloguing in Publication Data
A catalogue record for this book is available from the British Library

Back cover: painting by Walter Tyndale.

Set in 11.5/13 pt Minion by Beamreach Printing (www.beamreachuk.co.uk)
Printed and bound by Henry Ling Ltd, at the Dorset Press, Dorchester, DT1 1HD

Contents

This book is dedicated to my children, my wife Ros
and the Mill Street Memories Group.

*Author royalties from this book are being shared between
the Women's Refuge and Mill Street Housing Society.*

Foreword

Social History is a specialised study within the general theme of History, and it presents its own attractions, its own peculiar problems and its own very important contribution.

In this book on Mill Street, Dorchester, David Forrester shows the great interest that can be found in a detailed investigation of a small and unique community over the last 150 years. Separate from Dorchester, and even separate from its Manor of Fordington, Mill Street and its environs were for many years a place of deprivation, vice and crime, best avoided. In the circumstances, much of its history is undocumented. Only when upright citizens of the County Town began to recognise and deal with the problems of a neglected underclass, were enough documents created to serve as valid historic evidence.

However, another vital historical resource survives, though it is rapidly diminishing. David has made extensive and effective use of human memory stretching back through the twentieth century. Of course memory is fallible and not every detail may be absolutely accurate, but the vital ingredient is impression. The wealth of feeling evident in the words of those who were there creates an emotional atmosphere that brings home a vivid picture of a different world.

Walk through Mill Street today and be amazed at the contrast with the revealed recent past of less than a couple of generations ago. This book is indeed a most valuable contribution to our Social History. David deserves our congratulations and gratitude.

Terry Hearing
Local author, historian and Rotarian

Preface

'People talk about Mill Street, but every town had an area like that, it had to have, because it was where the poor lived.'

'Beware, keep away, don't you dare go there!' It's 1950 and you wouldn't expect part of Fordington in the county town of Dorchester to be 'out of bounds'. However, Mill Street had a reputation. And despite many changes for the better, this reputation was not easy to shake off.

By 1950 the lawlessness that had existed for over a century in Mill Street had almost faded away, helped by education in the Mill Street Mission and the schools. The age-old suspicions, however, were still there; they would remain until the residents were rehoused away from Mill Street in the early 1960s.

For the lads of Fordington, being told somewhere was 'out of bounds' just promoted it as a challenge. But Mill Street stood between us boys in Fordington and all the places of adventure that we wanted to reach. To a certain extent of course we respected what our parents said, and, when it was necessary to take a short cut through Mill Street, we did not hang about. From Holloway Road we went down the steps to the little bridge over the mill stream; crossing the bridge, we would then break into a trot through Hardy Avenue to Kings Road. From here we felt safe and would travel onward to Grey's Bridge and beyond to either Bockhampton or in the other direction across the field to the river 'swimming baths' or Pigeon Copse further on.

'It had a reputation as being a rough area, and kids were told to steer clear of them. I don't remember any friends in Mill Street. It's strange really, almost like a separate part of town.'

In this book I hope to transport you back to the beginning of the twentieth century to let you experience, through the memories of those who lived in Mill Street, what life was like in a not very advantaged part of Dorchester, where to a certain extent you were judged by what had gone before.

To myself and other like-minded people, it is important that this part of our local history is recorded, before it is lost forever down the mill stream.

'I don't know where people got that it was a place to be afraid of.'

Acknowledgements

Without the help of family, friends and acquaintances this book would not have been possible and I would like to thank the following. My wife Ros, who had to suffer my moods as things went wrong and encouraged me to continue. Terry Hearing, local historian, fellow Rotarian and friend. Rupert Edwards and Judith Dearlove, so helpful with information and pictures of old Mill Street. The Memories Project Group, Alec Bailey, John Smith, Kathryn Gould, Julia Gibbs, Allan Bailey, Linda House, Frank Voss and Sue Masters, all of whom have worked long and hard to record memories of Mill Street.

Thanks to all those who attended our open afternoons and passed on snippets of information, all of which make this book what it is.

Louise Pounds for painstakingly typing all the recordings. Jon Callan (window restorer), Nick Morris (designer, Wallis Agency) and Alfie Otton (for wonderful sketches). The Rev Dr John Travell for giving me letters and information left by his late wife's grandfather W.J. Fare. David Holden for supplying pictures and information. David Moxom for nearly 70 years of friendship and help in my research, and Derek Pride, who pointed me in the right direction on several occasions.

Sometimes people stumble over what can only be described as 'treasure'. This was the case when boxes of glass slides were found in the garage of a family house by a member of the Edwards family. These would have originally been shown using a magic lantern, and indeed the picture below shows the lantern in action. These slides were painstakingly cleaned up and digitised by Colin Parr, a committee member, and his friend Lt Col B.W. Bell MBE, something for which we are very grateful.

Many of the photographs in this book are provided by Rupert Edwards and Julia Gibbs, grandchildren of A.H. Edwards, founder of the Mill Street Mission. I thank Rupert and Julia for access to, and the use of, these valuable pieces of our social history.

This window from the old Mission hut is being refurbished by Jon Callan and will be placed on display in the Society's next new build.

Children attend a magic lantern show in the Mission Hall (pre 1940).

Introduction

As a boy, like others of my generation, we knew of the reputation of Mill Street and the fact that it was a place to be avoided. However, of its history we knew little. Indeed, it is true to say that until now, when I am in my seventies and have felt moved to write this book, I still knew little. The research carried out by myself and the group of willing helpers headed by Rupert Edwards and Judith Dearlove has uncovered so many facts and stories, which were unknown to me and probably most people who pick up this book.

I find it strange that at school (Dorchester Boys School) the history we were taught covered the Gorbals in Glasgow and how poor conditions were there, how tough things were and how much crime there was. However, was there any mention of Mill Street? No, not a word, yet on our doorstep was an area where the housing density and conditions were actually worse than the Gorbals.

The boys of Fordington were sitting on top of a chunk of history without knowing it.

Through this book, and by giving talks to the public and also at schools, I hope that we can put this right. Read on ... I think there will be some surprises in store.

As a Fordington boy I have two heroes. They are the Reverend Henry Moule and Alfred Edwards – the reasons for which will soon become clear.

Mill Street c 1914.

The History of Mill Street

The history of Mill Street is a chequered one. It was a place of hiding for those in distress or debt; and people living there in the early years included some of the dregs of society. They lived, if we can call it that, in houses packed tightly together, in tiny lanes, either side of the river (the Mill Stream), which was thoroughly polluted.

The houses were dank, overcrowded, rat-infested and mostly built on land that was below the level of the river. On bad days the filthy water would seep up through the flag-stone floors. There were no facilities and no room to rid oneself of rubbish or effluent; therefore they lived on top of it. Disease was rife, the area rarely being free from cholera and typhoid. In his old age, Moule told of 13 houses being served by one privy. On one night in a storm, Moule was kneeling by the bed of a dying man when a stream of effluent ran between him and the man on the bed.

'My wife admits that she was told to hold her nose and run past.'

'There was hundreds of them! Every house had mouse traps and things like that.'

'Sleeping was difficult, until you got used to the sound of the rats – they nested in the walls and thatch.'

Mill Stream and homes backing onto it, looking up towards Holloway Road.

Later, during the slum clearance of 1912, these houses at the bottom of Fordington were demolished.

The local press of the time reported on conditions in Mill Street.

Dorset County Chronicle, 1854

The Poor at our Gates

At the end of St George's Road, where Fordington meets its water meadows, you will find the local sewage works. Well, they have to be somewhere, one supposes – and Fordington has been the traditional site for the effluent of the town in times past. But there is a certain aptness about the location, considering St George's most famous vicar not only fought to improve sanitation of his parishioners, but was also a pioneer in the development of the earth-closet itself.

1848 Board of Health Report

... in High Fordington, from want of means of cleansing, typhus fever has not been absent for the last three years, and in Lower Fordington there is a crowded and pauper population dwelling in the midst of filth.

Rev Moule was the vicar of Fordington from 1829 until his death in 1880. His was the largest and poorest of Dorchester's four parishes.

> ### Dorset County Chronicle, 21 September 1854
> At the east end of Dorchester 1,100 people are congregated in a set
> of buildings, many of which are in the most wretched condition utterly
> destitute of the normal conveniences of life. The population consists
> of Labourers and Paupers, from this and many other parishes. Vice, in
> its worse forms, abounds amongst them. This space really consists of
> Mill Street on one side of the mill pond and Holloway Row, Cuckold
> Row, Standfast and Milk Street on the other. Most of the houses have
> no ground other than that on which they stand. Consequently their filth
> is cast either into the open or into the river or mill pond from which
> most people draw their water for washing and even sometimes for culinary
> purposes.

Amazingly, by 1853 cases of cholera had dropped and things seemed a little better. However, this was about to change as the very next year, in 1854, Mill Street became the centre of a raging cholera outbreak. Much of this was blamed not on the rat-infested living conditions of the area, but on the government's decision to house inmates from overcrowded Millbank Prison, in Pimlico, London, in Dorchester Barracks.

Dorchester Infantry Barracks, home of the Dorsetshire Regiment. The long building (centre) is the Little Keep. (Taken from Brian Bates Dorchester Remembers the Great War, courtesy of Dorset County Museum.)

These were empty due to the Dorsets being away fighting the Crimean War, and the government took the decision to use the space, choosing only those inmates who were thought to be free from cholera. Yet just 2 miles away from the Prison, in Soho, there was a severe outbreak of cholera (known as 'the Broad Street cholera outbreak'), and unfortunately cholera was also rife in Millbank.

They should have known that all the best-laid plans go wrong. Total segregation between prisoners in the Barracks and the rest of the population of Dorchester was promised. The importance of separation was stressed to

Dorset County Chronicle, 11 August 1854

The town was thrown into a state of great excitement, on Thursday afternoon, in consequence of a report that the Government intended to use the Dorchester barracks as a depot to house such inmates from Millbank who are thought to be free from the cholera, which now rages in that establishment. The Mayor (George Andrews, Esq.), at the request of the Municipal Body and inhabitants, proceeded to London, to represent the case to the Secretary of State; and, on Friday afternoon, pursuant to a requisition, the senior Alderman, Christopher Arden, Esq., called a public meeting of the inhabitants, which was held in the Town Hall.

the Mayor, who agreed to ensure that all contact would be prohibited. This, however, was not to last long.

On 24 August Rev Moule was on one of his routine visits to the area when he discovered that two women in Holloway Row had been contracted to wash clothes for the prisoners. The huge number of articles, dirty bedding, clothes and underwear filled him with dismay – five articles per man from 700 prisoners, a total of 3500 pieces, to be washed in two tiny cottages with no facilities whatsoever. Moule contacted the Mayor immediately, and he warned of the danger of cholera; however, this fell on deaf ears. Within days, a child living nearby was taken ill and died of cholera. This was only the first of many in the next month; 29 more deaths were recorded, all within a short distance of the cottages where the washing was carried out. Two things were clear: the men's outer clothing was new but their bedding and underwear had come from cholera-ridden Millbank. It was obvious that the infection had travelled in the soap suds down the open gutters that ran between the cottages. Moule, who with his wife had worked for 18 hours a day during this period, was filled with grief that he had failed to halt this epidemic.

Another possible cause of the spread of the disease was that the cottages were frequented by prison warders, though this was strictly forbidden by the authorities: 'Nay, in the very house in which on Thursday 31st August, the second case occurred, and in which there have been three cases and two deaths, one of these men was drinking and passing a portion of the previous Tuesday night', reported Moule at the time. The men were probably desperate for company, and one has to remember that in Mill Street there was a row of cottages called Cuckold Row (a *cuckold* is the husband of an adulteress, often regarded as an object of derision). So Cuckold Row may have been just the place that a lonely man far from home would go to seek female company.

Clearly fed up with the way things were going, and being exhausted (with both him and his wife working 18 hours a day), Rev Moule was moved to write the following to HRH Prince Albert on 21 September 1854:

May it please your Royal Highness,

God has in His providence again visited this unhappy parish with cholera in its most frightful form. And as the parish is one of the estates of the Duchy of Cornwall and your Royal Highness is the President of the council of the Duchy, I am constrained by feelings and convictions which I cannot resist, to bring the case and matters connected with it immediately and fully before your notice. I must write in the few intervals of rest from almost incessant attention to the sick. Of the immediate cause of its introduction amongst us I have my opinion, and I shall not hesitate to express it. But the main subject, on which I venture thus to address your Highness, is that of the circumstances through which this and other epidemics, when once introduced into a portion of this parish, are fostered and aggravated. And my excuse for the liberty I thus take, is the conviction long since felt, but strengthened as during the last twelve days I have passed from house to house of the sick and dying, that while the blame of those circumstances is to be attributed in part to others, no inconsiderable portion of it lies at the door of those who for the last sixty or seventy years have managed this estate of his Royal Highness the Duke of Cornwall. For they when they might have prevented it, allowed such a state of things to grow up, partly it is true on a piece of freehold land, but that surrounded on all sides by his Royal Highness's property, and inhabited in part by labourers on his estate; and for the twenty five years of my incumbency the council has never stretched forth a hand even to alleviate this state of things. Yet in their power it is, and, as I believe, in their power alone, to apply to it an effectual and permanent remedy.

This letter was acknowledged and was reported in the *Chronicle* (on 21 September 1854), as was a second letter. However, nothing changed. It is easy to read into this letter the tiredness and frustration felt by Moule.

Slum conditions in the cottages allowed the fever to spread rapidly, but the activities of Rev Moule helped to prevent it reaching the population of nearby Dorchester. In October 1854 a Testimonial Subscription was raised, to present a framed Testimonial Certificate to 'the Reverend Henry and

The Reverend Henry Moule and Mrs Moule.

Clusters of damp, dilapidated houses of wattle and daub were owned by small landlords who rented them by the room, with up to a dozen people of all ages crammed into a single room.

Mrs Moule whose self-denying labours and unremitting exertions during the visitation of cholera in September 1854 are thus gratefully acknowledged by the inhabitants of Fordington and the neighbourhood'.

The Burial Record of St George's Church in Fordington shows that 30 people between the ages of 2 and 69 died between 1 and 26 September 1854. It would seem that people accepted this as a fact of life, and indeed life in Mill Street went on, as we shall hear in the next chapter.

The Mill Street Mission

Alfred Harman Edwards was a member of a well-to-do family of accountants. However, in 1905, aged just 19, he recognised many of the problems that existed in Mill Street, and was the driving force behind efforts to start an interdenominational mission (the Mill Street Mission) to cater for the spiritual and material needs of Dorchester's poor.

'Mr Edwards was a good man, very kind; he did a lot for Mill Street and the children.'

When Mr Edwards came into the room all the boys immediately sat still and crossed their arms, as a mark of respect.

Each year the Mission had a different motto.

The Mission was based in a pair of old thatched cottages in Mill Street below the ridge on which Fordington's ancient parish church of St George's sits.

The cottages were replaced in 1929 by a larger brick building, together with a corrugated-iron hut that became the Mission Hall.

The original home of the Mission at No. 57 Mill Street.

Mrs Williams, a founder member of the Mill Street Housing Society, opens the new Mission.

Children admiring the new Mission building.

Imagine the bravery required for someone of Edwards' age and background to step into this den of iniquity. Thomas Hardy called the place Mixen Lane in his novel *The Mayor of Casterbridge* and describes it thus in Chapter 36:

A crowded street. The Mission (not yet in existence in this photo) was housed in the thatched terrace on the left; Churchill's mill is visible on the right in the background.

Mixen Lane was the Adullam of all the surrounding villages. It was the hiding-place of those who were in distress, and in debt, and trouble of every kind. Farm-labourers and other peasants, who combined a little poaching with their farming, and a little brawling and bibbing with their poaching, found themselves sooner or later in Mixen Lane. Rural mechanics too idle to mechanize, rural servants too rebellious to serve, drifted or were forced into Mixen Lane.

The lane and its surrounding thicket of thatched cottages stretched out like a spit into the moist and misty lowland. Much that was sad, much that was low, some things that were baneful, could be seen in Mixen Lane. Vice ran freely in and out certain of the doors in the neighbourhood; recklessness dwelt under the roof with the crooked chimney; shame in some bow-windows; theft (in times of privation) in the thatched and mud-walled houses by the sallows. Even slaughter had not been altogether unknown here. In a block of cottages up an alley there might have been erected an altar to disease in years gone by. Such was Mixen Lane in the times when Henchard and Farfrae were Mayors.

Behind the Mission building, with the green tin-hut building in the background.

This hut was used as the Mission Hall and was originally in the yard of the Mission house. It was later taken down and removed to Broadmayne where it was used as a scout hut.

Under Alfred's leadership, the Mission provided a soup kitchen and gave away food and clothing; it also ran a bath house with hot water and clothes washing facilities

'Mr Edwards built the bath house; we used to take it in turns – so many girls, then so many boys.'

Behind the Mission. The bath house was on the left (not seen in this picture).

'Well, the boys had a way of climbing on the bath-house roof, they would make little holes and they could look down and see you.'

Bible readings and prayer services were held in the new Mission. Note the segregation of women and children on one side, men on the other. The men had to remove their hats, while women kept theirs on.

Regular prayer meetings and scripture readings were held. The Mission also provided a Youth Fellowship, Men's Club and Mother's Meeting, and taught girls sewing and cooking, and boys scouting.

Mr Edwards also took over the maintenance of the German War Memorial in St George's churchyard, and the Mission scouts helped look after it.

Even the unemployed were looked after. At the Unemployed Club, men

Girls' sewing class, with Mrs E. Dodd and Dora Bird.

THE BOY SCOUTS ASSOCIATION.

25, BUCKINGHAM PALACE ROAD,

LONDON, S. W. 1.

26th. December, 1925.

Dear Colonel,

I am so pleased to see that the Dorchester Boy Scouts have been placing wreaths on the Memorial to German prisoners, buried during the War in the cemetery there.

It speaks to a very good spirit, and the one that we want to develop; namely, that whatever may have been the conflict of feelings between the past generation of British and Germans, it would be a crime if we brought up the oncoming races to dislike each other for the sins of their fathers.

This seems to have been a really practical step in the direction of goodwill towards those who were our enemies in the past, and I am very glad to see the Dorchester boys leading the way in that direction.

Believe me,

Yours truly,

Robert S. aden Power

The Mission Scouts troop, which took over from the Boys Life Brigade.

Above and below: Activities at the Unemployed Club, 1929–30.

Boys Life Brigade marching past the Swan Inn. Mr T.F. Scudder was the leader in those days.

learned handicrafts and mending shoes – no one was left idle. But it wasn't all work – there were also carol parties, keep fit and football matches.

With his softly, softly approach, this gradually proved to be a huge success; people began to see the light and many felt a great weight lifted from their shoulders. As for the children, they suddenly had a focus, and a base where they

Christmas party at the Mission.

felt safe as never before. There was a great regard felt for the teachers and helpers, which remained with people for the rest of their lives. Talking to many older folk who attended the Mission, they speak so warmly of the people and the times they had, remembering vividly names and the lessons learnt.

'Having the Mill Street Mission was a blessing to all of us. We always felt that when we went to the Mission it was a fun day. We could probably say that we were learning more than we learned anywhere else.'

How lucky can we be with a trip to Swanage.

Nothing is remembered with more joy than the summer outing. These were children who had very little and certainly did not go on holiday. Therefore the trip by train to Weymouth or Swanage, the day on the beach with others, whatever the weather, the freedom, fresh air and fun lasted long in the memory. This was followed by tea in the local church hall, made by the Mission ladies; especially remembered were the orange squash and Marmite sandwiches. Not a banquet by today's standards, but remembered long by those who attended.

Adults pose for a photo during a trip to Weymouth.

The Mill Street Housing Society

Despite the good work of the Mill Street Mission, by 1931 things had improved very little. The 1912 slum clearance had had limited impact on conditions in Mill Street, so a group of people led by Alfred Edwards and Florence Hardy (the widow of the author Thomas Hardy) decided to form the Mill Street Housing Society. This was registered as a limited company on 16 October 1931. It was only the sixth such housing association in the country. Mrs Hardy, JP, was the first Chairman, with A.H. Edwards the Secretary, together with a committee of six.

On the programme (overleaf) produced for the laying of the foundation stone it is interesting to note the names of the VIPs involved. The list of local businessmen as First Members was obviously meant to show what a worthy cause this was and to encourage more people to invest.

Dorset County Chronicle, 26 November 1931

The Mill Street Mission began in a small way and in very humble surroundings, but it seems destined to accomplish something very much bigger than its founders ever anticipated. In founding the Mission 26 years ago they founded better than they knew. How could they have known that a quarter of a century afterwards the Mission would have given birth to a great social enterprise like the Mill St Housing Society Ltd, which has just been registered under the Industrial and Providential Societies Acts and whose prospectus appears elsewhere.

It is a sign of the times; it meets one of the definite needs of the times; it sets out boldly to emancipate some of the dwellers who live in dwellings which endanger their health and sour their whole lives. To improve housing conditions in the way that Mill St Housing Society proposes is to engage in one of our greatest social services and it is a project which the public can have a hand in as well. It means building up a new social life for a very deserving class of citizens who are entitled by all the laws of justice and morality to live under decent conditions. The Society is not necessarily competing with corporate housing schemes.

The Mill Street Housing Society, Ltd.

(Registered Pursuant to the Industrial and Provident Society's Acts, 1893 to 1928 , on October 16th, 1931)

Registered No. 11354 R. Dorset

President :
COLONEL SIR ROBERT WILLIAMS BART.

Chairman of Committee :
MRS. THOMAS HARDY, J.P.

Committee :

MRS. A. R. CAVE	CAPT. A. H. CHRISTIE, M.C.
MISS E. A. EMERY	MR. W. J. FARE, J.P.
MISS W. MARSDEN, O.B.E.	MR. A. J. ROSSITER, J.P.
MISS EVELYN WILLIAMS	MR. E. W. TILLEY, J.P.

Architect :
MR. SYDNEY A. JACKSON, L.R.I.B.A.

Auditors :
MESSRS. THOS. A. PEARCE AND CLAYTON
Chartered Accountants.

Hon. Secretary :
MR. A. H. EDWARDS
Registered Office—22 HIGH EAST STREET,
DORCHESTER

Laying of the Foundation Stone

ON

Wednesday, June 1st, 1932

---

*"Be it ever so humble,
There's no place like home."*

THE MILL STREET HOUSING SOCIETY LTD.

FIRST SCHEME
Contractor—W. J. GUPPY
DORCHESTER

Laying of the Foundation Stone

Wednesday, June 1st, 1932

HIS WORSHIP THE MAYOR OF DORCHESTER
(Mr. COUNCILLOR W. J. FARE, J.P.)
will preside

Prayer by the Mayor's Chaplain
(Rev. ANDREW LEGGATT)

" Except the Lord build the house, they labour in vain that build it :
except the Lord keep the city, the watchman waketh but in vain."
—*Psalm* 127 i.

Apologies for absence and messages of goodwill from

COL. SIR ROBERT WILLIAMS, BART. (President of the Society).

W. J. BRYMER, ESQ., J.P. (High Sheriff of the County of Dorset).

MAJOR H. P. NICHOLSON (Chairman of the Public Health and Housing Committee, Dorset County Council).

MRS. V. M. HIRST.

MR. COUNCILLOR F. C. JAMES, J.P., C.C.

HIS WORSHIP THE MAYOR will speak.

MR. S. A. JACKSON, L.R.I.B.A., (the Society's Architect) will present a Mallet, made of oak taken from the old Mill Street Mission premises, and invite—

MRS. THOMAS HARDY, J.P. (Chairman of the Society) to lay the Foundation Stone. Mrs. Hardy will declare the stone well and truly laid, and will speak.

Greetings will be expressed by—

MISS COUNCILLOR W. MARSDEN, O.B.E. (on behalf of the Women's Institute)

MR. COUNCILLOR A. J. ROSSITER, J.P. (Vice Chairman Housing Committee)

A. J. PALLETT, ESQ., (President Dorchester Rotary Club)

MR. COUNCILLOR A. R. JEFFERY (President Dorchester and District Chamber of Commerce)

A resolution of THANKS will be proposed by

MRS. A. R. CAVE ; seconded by

MR. COUNCILLOR E. W. TILLEY, J.P.

" It is not too much to say that an adequate solution of the housing question is the foundation of all social progress. Health and housing are indissolubly connected. If this country is to be the country which we desire to see it become, a great offensive must be undertaken against disease and crime and the first point at which the attack must be delivered is the unhealthy, ugly, overcrowded houses in the mean street, which we all of us know too well."
—Speech of His Majesty the King at Buckingham Palace.

That the Minister of Health recognises the value of the voluntary housing movement is clear from the following extract from Ministry of Health Official Circular No. 1024 :—

" The need for more houses, especially for the less well paid members of the community, is still great, and the Minister trusts that, as a result of the alteration of the Order of 1928 referred to in this Circular, Local Authorities will take every possible step, by the development of their own programmes and by the encouragement of public utility societies and other bodies who are willing to work under conditions of the 1924 Act, to ensure that there shall be a steady increase in the number of houses available for letting."

THE MILL STREET HOUSING SOCIETY, Ltd.

I enclose cheque or cash for the sum of ....

(1) As a Donation.

(2) As payment for £1 Ordinary Shares.

(3) As payment for Loan Stock.

(Please strike out the words which do not apply).

Name in Full (block capitals)......................................

Address ....

Usual Signature......................................

(Bankers : Westminster Bank Ltd.)

Indeed the prospectus makes it clear when it says; there is still a great need for healthy accommodation among those who cannot afford the rent of the excellent houses provided by the council.

The Society therefore proposes, subject to the necessary finance being forthcoming, to build houses or flats at the lowest possible rents. It also wants to do other equally important things in such matters, and that is to recondition existing premises wherever it is practicable. Although there are a lot of houses that ought to be razed to the ground, there are others which the best brains of the architect and builder can be turned into very habitable dwellings and this is being done all over England. Voluntary service has been placed at the disposal of the Society, which enables it to do without any management salaries and to keep overhead charges to the lowest possible figure ... .

The public are invited to do one of three things or all three: 1. Send a gift of money. 2. Purchase £1 ordinary shares which carries no dividend, but the holder of one share becomes a member and controls the management by right to vote. 3. Subscribe for 2½% loan stock, on which dividends will be paid half yearly, and the amount repaid in 40 years.

His Majesty the King once said that "the first point of the attack in the great offensive against disease and crime must be the unhealthy, ugly, and overcrowded houses in the mean street".

The Mill Street Housing Society Ltd has launched its campaign, and better still has disclosed its plans. It is something in the nature of a great adventure, too, but the rewards will come presently in a regenerated social life in healthier and happier homes.

It is clear that the above did not fall on deaf ears, as by 30 January 1932 plans were well ahead on the building of the first houses in Kings Road and preparations for the laying of the foundation stone were being made.

Meanwhile Mrs Hardy was worried that when they moved families into new, more healthy properties, the old property they had vacated would become packed with yet more unfortunates. Thus moved, she wrote a letter to the Mayor (reproduced overleaf courtesy of Rev Dr John Travell). The letter is very polite, failing of course to mention that Mr Fare was one of the first shareholders and well aware of what was going on! They were after all both Justices of the Peace, sitting on the bench together; indeed they became JPs on the same day. This letter was very obviously aimed at the Council as a whole, signed by Secretary A.H. Edwards, Chairman Florence

Hardy and President Col Sir Robert Williams to add weight, they being three of the foremost citizens of Dorchester at the time.

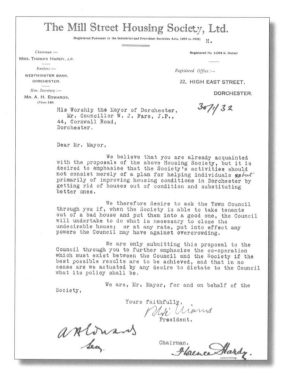

So we move on to the great day – 1 June 1932, the laying of the official Foundation Stone of the first houses in Kings Road. All the important people of Dorchester were there, and the Mayor gave the following speech (reproduced here courtesy of Rev Dr John Travell):

We meet here today in the interest of good housing, to lay the foundation stone of the first house to be erected under the Mill Street Housing Society. May it be the first of a large number?

In presiding at this ceremony, I should like to say that you have the sympathy and practical help of the Town Council in what we believe can be a very useful contribution towards the solution of a very difficult problem.

The need for better houses in the district is acute, and we know that this Society has arisen as a direct result of careful constant observation, of those keenly interested in the welfare of the residents in this part of the town.

We appeal to all those who are desirous of bettering the conditions of the homes of our people, to come forward and lend a hand in so worthy a cause, by either lending money at a low rate of interest, or by taking ordinary shares.

Whilst the various housing schemes carried out by the Town Council have been of great assistance in comfortably housing as many families as houses built, there is still an urgent need for more of the type being commenced today.

The success of this undertaking, and its extension in further building, must depend on those members of the public who can render practical help in the manner already suggested.

We are glad to have as our Chairman Mrs Thomas Hardy, who has shown great interest in the foundation of the Society, and we are glad she is able to be here today to lay the first Foundation Stone.

In Mr A.H. Edwards (our Secretary) we have a gentleman of proved ability, and in him we have the utmost confidence, knowing that whatever he puts his hand to will be carried out with that efficiency which is so characteristic of him.

To his foresight and energy, the establishment of this Society is largely due, and we follow its history with every good wish and prayer, that through such agency many families will be better housed, and, being better housed, they may indeed prove more useful citizens in regard to health and general good character, and ultimate happiness.

Many prominent townsfolk have already come forward and associated themselves with the Society, which is of great encouragement, and their sympathy is much appreciated.

I now have much pleasure in asking Mrs Thomas Hardy to lay this foundation stone.

Laying the foundation stone of the first Mill Street Society houses in Kings Road, with the Mayor and Mayoress and Mrs Hardy (right of the stone).

The foundations of a highly successful building programme were thus laid and significant progress was made in the years ahead. Below is a précis of the principal events and achievements of the Society over the next 65 years.

1931   The Society was formed under the Industrial and Provident Societies Act 1893 (Amendment 1928).

Building in Kings Road – they were all built with flat concrete roofs. W. Guppy was the builder and S.A. Jackson the architect.

Hardy Avenue houses – from building site to finished homes.

1932 The first four three-bedroom homes were built in Kings Road, for which the contract stipulated that part of the workforce should be local.

1933 The next six three-bedroom houses were built in Kings Road.

1934 Eight houses were built in Hardy Avenue.

1936 Seventeen old cottages in Mill Street were purchased and modernised.

1938 Four self-contained flats were built in Hardy Avenue.

1940 The old roller flour mill at the foot of St George's churchyard was turned into nine flats and a shop. It retains the name The Old Mill.

The old flour mill – before and after renovations. (Sketch courtesy of Alfie Otton.)

1941 Another old cottage was purchased and renovated.

1942 The Old Vicarage at the top of High Street Fordington (home of Rev Moule and family) was acquired and converted into five flats. (Thomas Hardy used to visit the Vicarage regularly, as the vicar's second son, Horace, befriended young Hardy.)

Inside the mill during renovations.

1943 Nine cottages in Mill Street were purchased.

1944 A cottage at Charminster was bought.

1946   Stables adjoining the Old Mill were converted into two houses.

1947   One house in Kings Road was purchased.

1948   Nos 25–27 and 37–38 Mill Street and 60 High Street Fordington were purchased and virtually rebuilt.

Nos 25–27 Mill Street, the only original cottages still remaining today. It is believed that one of them used to be a bakery. (Sketch by Alfie Otton.)

1948/9 Five homes for ex-servicemen were built with proceeds of subscriptions to the Dorset Regiment's War Memorial fund. These regimental houses (two in Sherborne, one in Upton, Poole, one in Broadmayne, and one in Dorchester) were named to commemorate battles of the Second World War at which the Dorsets were awarded medals.

1950   Two more cottages in Mill Street were purchased.

1951   Maurice Edwards took over the work following his father's death.

The Edwards family, with (right) three generations of Edwards men.

1952   At a meeting in November, the redevelopment of Mill Street was considered for the first time.

1953   Deeds of the five Dorset Regiment War Memorial Homes were finally transferred to the Society.

Work commences.

1954/6 A general programme of modernisation and improvement of the older properties was undertaken.

1958   Five cottages at the eastern end of Mill Street were sold to the Town Council for demolition and subsequent development of land.

1959   The Old Vicarage flats were modernised.

1960   Eighteen cottages in the centre of Mill Street were sold to the Town Council for redevelopment.

1961   A new Dorset Regiment War Memorial House was built at The Grove, Dorchester, from the proceeds of the sale of the Broadmayne house.

1963   The house in Glyde Path Road was sold.

1964   The Society now owned 38 houses, 29 flats and 4 bungalows.

1964   Twelve self-contained flats known as Mill Stream House were completed and formally opened by Her Majesty's Lord Lieutenant for Dorset, Colonel Sir Joseph Weld.

1967   Plans were initiated to demolish the Old Vicarage and replace it with another 12 self-contained flats and a communal area in three blocks, to be known as Fordington Hill House.

1972   Fordington Hill House was formally opened by Councillor Leslie Phillips.

1973   Nine garages were built on land in Holloway Road opposite The Old Mill.

1978   The four flats in Hardy Avenue were substantially improved and enlarged.

1982   Extensive enlargement and modernisation of the Old Mill planned, to create 17 self-contained flats.

1984   The Housing Corporation granted a long-term mortgage to the Society.

1987   The Old Mill was rebuilt and formally reopened by the Director of the National Federation of Housing Associations, Mr Richard Best (of Godmanston). A plaque tracing the history of the mill was installed, together with the stained-glass window commemorating both World Wars taken from the original Mill Street Mission property.

The war memorial window in the Old Mill.

1989   Extensive modernisation of all Kings Road and Hardy Avenue properties began.

1990   The Mill Street Mission was formally dissolved, and a Deed of Gift transferred ownership of its last remaining asset, No. 15 South Walks Road, to the Society.

1991　To comply with Housing Corporation requirements over possible conflict of interests, Maurice Edwards ceded his voting right in a committee post, and was elected President of the Society.

1993　Three old properties in Mill Street were demolished and seven three-bedroom houses were built in their stead, known as Edwards Court.

1995　West Dorset District Council generously helped renovate Nos 25, 26 and 27 Mill Street. The last of the 1931 2.5% Loan Stock was repaid to the heirs of the subscribers.

1996　After Edwards Court, no more new houses or flats were built, instead the Society choosing to buy on the open market and renting at affordable rents.

Edwards Court today.

The Society currently owns 87 properties, a mixture of flats and family homes. Forty flats provide sheltered housing and the Society employs a full-time Warden to help and support them. The Society continues to provide affordable housing in Fordington, true to its original aims set out in 1931:

'... to build houses or flats at the lowest possible rents. As is well known, there is still a great need for healthy accommodation among those who cannot afford the rent of the excellent houses provided by the Council. The Society will also endeavour to improve, where possible, any existing premises, if capable of acquisition on reasonable terms, and fit to be reconditioned. Where these are overcrowded, they can be re-let to smaller families, provided alternative accommodation is available for larger ones ... It is frankly admitted that the proposals may not be deemed to constitute a commercially attractive investment, but it is felt that there are sufficient people who are acutely aware of the evil effects of bad housing and who may be willing to thus assist in relieving this state of affairs.'

This is obviously a remarkable result, and shows that the caring aspect of the Society continues – something A.H. Edwards would be proud of.

That's the Way it Was

Much of what you read in the rest of the book is based on the memories of people born between 1917 and 1940. A working group was formed to contact and record the stories that Mill Street folk had to tell. Interestingly, there were significant similarities despite the considerable age differences.

One fact quickly became apparent – anyone born and brought up in Mill Street had the total and utter acceptance of 'that was the way it was'. No hard feelings, no thoughts of what might have been – that was their lot and they accepted it. It is amazing how often a sentence is finished with the words 'but they were happy times, we didn't mind, we just got on with it'.

'We wasn't jealous of anybody, because they never had anything either, did they?'

'I feel that life in Mill Street was good, as good as you could have got anywhere.'

'I remember the sweet factory, there was that wonderful smell that drifted over the fence.'

'So really life was how you made it, at the time we made it perfect, everybody joined in. We were all together, all helped each other.'

The children of Mill Street had very little, but there was little to have when compared with modern children and living today. The great thing children of that generation did have was freedom – the fields, woods and rivers were their playground, with no barriers; they were free to roam, build camps and play imaginary games, climb trees (sometimes to great heights), without restraint or protection, yet injury was rare. Fishing started at a young age, with a jam jar and a piece of string, progressing to trout tickling and then hook and hand-line, baited with bread paste. Avoiding the water bailiff was a skill learned early on and became part of the game, possibly enjoyed by both parties; indeed, bailiff and poacher often became firm friends, and when one bailiff, Mr Bowditch, died, many of those who attended his funeral in 2011 were former poachers.

'There was a footbridge by the Mill. When the river was low we would tie a

'Prince's Bridge, known to us boys as "Swan Bridge" as it was next to the Swan pub. After closing the lock gates to do some maintenance work on the river it was a good time for prodding about in the river bed, looking for eels under stones, to be served up for dinner in many homes.'

fork to a stick, lean over the bridge and try to stab the eels when they stuck their heads out from under the bridge.'

Play time – Richard Brown (right) and possibly Laurence Brown.

Many of the things enjoyed at that time included breaking the law, for example scrumping (stealing fruit, mainly apples). We didn't think of it as stealing, it was more of a game with an acceptable ending, as long as you were not caught or recognised. Recognition was worse as you then faced punishment from Father, who felt you had let the family down.

'If you were caught doing wrong a policeman may clip you around the earhole; if you told Dad he would give you another one and say you must have deserved it.'

I 'bags' is a word we would often use. In the 1940s and 50s, as children looked into a shop window at toys they could never hope to own, it was common to hear, 'I bags the red racing car' or 'I bags that crane'. That was the nearest most would ever get to owning such things, but for one brief moment in time the toys were 'theirs'.

One sad story involved a lad who, like most, had very few toys but loved a boat that was in French's (the paper and toy shop in High East Street). Now he really wanted this boat, so his mother paid six pence a week into the Christmas Club. Just imagine his surprise on Christmas Day to actually be given this boat. Friends came round on Christmas morning and soon two boys were off to the river, the boat in their hands tied to a piece of string. At the river the proud owner launched the boat and it floated along in the strong current. The other lad, wanting a go, made a grab for the string, which slipped through both their hands, setting the boat free. The little boat speeded off downriver and disappeared under the mill. The boys rushed to the other side, but waited in vain for it to reappear. One can only imagine the pain a loss like this must have caused to those who had so little. Do children today value things in the same way?

At that time, little did the lad who lost the boat know that the river was destined to bring him yet more pain. What follows are his own words:

'By sad coincidence, my grandmother went in the same way, years later in the 1960s. My mother's mother, she fell in the river by Swanbridge Caravan Park, and went down through the river, under the mill and she finished up at Louds Mill …I found her with two of my mates on a Sunday morning, when the police arranged a search. I had been searching all week for her, strangely enough; I was her only grandson or grand-daughter that took time off work to look for her. I took my mother and a couple of aunties all around Cerne Abbas where she lived for a long time, looked everywhere, and then the police arranged an official search. I said to the chap in charge, "I'm going down to Louds Mill". Two of the chaps I worked with came with me. We went over this little wooden bridge, I remember flats that used to be there. We split up and soon they shouted, "We have found her". I wanted to look but they stopped me, it wasn't a pretty sight.'

Daily Life

In Mill Street the population density in 1900 was almost 500 per acre, higher than that of the Gorbals in Glasgow, which was 464.2 per acre. Daily life in Mill Street at the end of the 19th century was unlike anything we can imagine. For many, this life of daily drudgery was almost unbearable, especially for the women folk who had to get by on a pittance and were often blamed when there was not much on the table.

'I was about 11 or 12 when I was plucking chickens, we all did it. I left school at 14. My mother was a widow at 33, she was expecting my brother. The year before that she lost Billy; I didn't know him. I was about 10 months when my Dad died.'

'I used to wash between 400 and 500 milk bottles a day, as well as doing all the cleaning in the milk house and everything. My hands were all chapped from the soda water you see.'

'Then I went on to Adam's (plumbers) – just imagine, I was cycling Dorchester to Broadmayne and Martinstown on a push bike with loads of tools, fittings and goodness knows what.'

View across the meadows towards Louds Mill.

31

One big problem was that most men only had poorly paid casual work. It was usually in the fields and water meadows nearby, or in the markets. Some worked as 'drowners', which entailed keeping the water channels clear in the meadows ready for when they would be flooded (drowned) in winter.

Ten Hatches, above the 'swimming baths'.

This system of channels, weirs and hatches (small gates) to regulate the water levels was developed by Dutch engineers in the 17th century. They discovered that a small amount of water flowing across the soil kept the ground temperature up, so that grass could grow all year round. Water was diverted back into the river again when the meadow was needed for grazing. In Dorset, farmers kept sheep on the meadows between late February and March. Then they were flooded a second time to encourage the hay crop, after which the cattle were brought back in. For many years, this hay crop was very important as the 'meadow hay' contained many herbs and plants not found in hay from normal fields, and it was considered to be far superior by the horse trainers in Newmarket. Therefore the meadow hay could be sold, and a cheaper product was bought in for the cows, providing the farmer with a profit. However, as you can imagine this system was very labour intensive. When the cattle grazed the meadows, they inevitably trod the sides of the ditches in, especially when wet, creating extra work.

The system of hatches also served another purpose: the River Frome provided the power to drive the many mills in the area and it was divided into several streams to reach the likes of Friary Mill, West Mill, East Mill and Louds Mill.

Other work in the area was seasonal, such as haymaking, harvesting and thrashing. This work was jealously guarded as men tried to keep it in the family. The men were paid daily and unfortunately quite often returned home by way of the pub, where they spent much of their day's wages. Also, sadly, the pubs opened early and men would often call in for a flagon of beer or cider on their way to work. It was not unusual at that time to hear the words 'there's no dinner, your dad drank it' or 'if you want something to eat you'll have to thieve it'.

The Mill Street Mission, with Men's Club next door, aimed at keeping the men out of the pubs so they didn't spend all their wages on drink.

Those who worked at the market sometimes fared better, as, although still poorly paid, there was often a chance of a bonus in the form of a pail of milk. A farmer could take 2 days to walk his cow to market, so casual workers were given the job of milking the poor beast to relieve the pressure on her udder. Quite often, however, the cow would be sold with calf tied alongside, so the calf had a share. Many of the casual workers would take a pail (one of their most valuable possessions) to market in the hope of free milk. This milk then had to be carried all the way back to Fordington, without being spilt, or worse stolen.

Mill Street being well known as a most disreputable, ungovernable area was shunned by people in the rest of Fordington. It was always given a wide berth, children being warned to avoid the place. At its worst, Mill Street became internally self-governing, ruled by patriarchal families whose wealth, such as it was, came from the markets, and other things it is best not to mention. These families' words were law. Punishment was handed out on an ad-hoc basis. However, power often changed hands from generation to generation; nothing was forever. Outsiders were treated with suspicion, often shunned and asked to leave. Unless of course a use could be found for them! In which case they often wished they had left.

Things did not improve much after the turn of the 19th century. The words 'Law and Order' meant little to the inhabitants of Mill Street. It was hoped that with the start of 'Slum Clearance' in 1912 things would improve; however, as stated, in Mill Street little changed. The police were a rare sight and would never patrol the area alone. An Officer of the Law would wait at the White Hart Pub until joined by another, before venturing onward into Fordington and the Mill Street area in particular. Incredibly this was true right up until after the end of the Second World War.

Things being as they were in Mill Street, it was not uncommon for families to swap houses when one family was growing and another had older children who had flown the nest. Right up until the 1950s, no one expected a lot.

'We had no hot water, the outside tap froze in winter, so no water. No bedding hardly, we slept under an Army Greatcoat, very few clothes, mostly old and second or third hand. The only bedroom furniture was a bed, not even that sometimes, just a mattress, on the floor, no wardrobe or drawers, nothing to put in them, shoes or boots that didn't fit, with cardboard covering the holes in the bottom, but we were still a happy family and had some wonderful happy times.'

How many of our children today would suffer any of this and be happy?

'My brother and I shared a pair of shoes and they had cardboard in to cover the holes, so we only went to school every other day.'

'You had no hot water, you had to light a fire under the boiler with logs and coal, and then when it was hot tip it into the tin bath on the floor.'

'Then one day we moved up to Old Poundbury; the house had a toilet, a bath and hot and cold water – heaven, we couldn't believe it!'

Diet

As money was very short, subsequently diet was extremely poor. Milk and cheese were relatively cheap, and bread, cheese, potatoes and, occasionally, bacon (mostly fat) formed the basis of the working man's diet. Meat was a rarity, reserved for the middle classes. Families relied very much on relatives to help out when times were tough, which they almost always were; relatives who had a garden or allotment would often supply a few vegetables, which the family would eke out to last the week. People of all denominations, and none, could also rely on the church for bread and other handouts.

'We used to pickle everything or salt it down, shallots, red cabbage and beans.'

'You didn't feed the ducks; if you had any bread left over it went into bread pudding.'

'Grandad had an allotment. He used to shoot rooks with a catapult. When he killed one he would hang it on a stick in the middle of the plot, to keep others away. Sometimes there were two or three hanging there, they used to rot and smell, I hated that!'

'Grandad used to grow all the vegetables. When he had a break he would sit in the shed with a pipe and a glass of cider.'

'Mum was outside talking. A woman came by and said there was chocolate in a shop up the town, so they both grabbed their Ration Books and rushed up the town. That's how it was in those days.'

Playtime

One huge difference between children years ago and modern-day children was their inventiveness. Children then would invent games, places and situations out of next to nothing. A few old boxes and a tablecloth became a house, a palace or a dungeon, and to them it all seemed real.

Another difference in Fordington was the state of the pavements – they were always covered in chalk marks. Lumps of chalk being readily available, children made good use of it. Hop-scotch squares were drawn on the pavements everywhere. Also arrows in chalk appeared daily; a person would be selected to run off, leaving chalk arrows to show where he had gone down alleys, even over walls. After counting to one hundred the others would attempt to chase him down. It all sounds simple, but what fun we had. If you were really quick you could run a distance, then double back and hide, and thus get the thrill of watching those who were pursuing you go running past; no wonder children then kept fit and slim. When drawing lots to see who went first, we held out a clenched fist, tapping each person's fist and chanting 'one potato, two potato, three potato, four, five potato, six potato, seven potato, more, O U T spells out, and out you must go'; this continued until there was only one person left, the chosen one.

Chalk was also used for another reason. Where there was a space and a brick wall a set of cricket stumps would be drawn, then let the game begin! However, the lack of proper stumps and bales often led to arguments about being out – did the ball really hit the stumps? Was there chalk on the ball? Was that chalk on the ball from when it hit the stumps the time before? Oh, the arguments could be endless.

The great lack of equipment led to coats or jumpers being used: in football they were the goal posts, with the inevitable arguments about whether the ball went over the imaginary bar or under, in which case it was a goal. When playing rounders you ran around a ring of coats or jumpers. The other ever-present articles were skipping ropes, hoops, five stones, a football of sorts (often past its best and semi-inflated) and cricket ball (very old and made of what appeared to be solid cork, very hard and prone to inflicting injuries).

A homemade catapult and bow and arrows were two other pieces of equipment that often sent you home early with some form of injury. Many of the things children did years ago would never be attempted now. Lads really did fire arrows, some with nails in the end, at one another. On one occasion, boys witnessed a lad peep around a tree only to have an arrow hit him in the corner of the eye and hang there. A blood-shot eye was the result, but it could have been much worse. Bruises from stones and even ball bearings fired from catapults were a common injury.

A homemade banger comprised an old key, hollowed at the top, with a nail fitted in the hole; string was tied at one end to the key and one to the nail; tips of red-top matches, readily available years ago, were broken off and inserted in the hole in the key end and the nail inserted also into the key end, which was then swung by the string hard against the wall, nail first. According to how many match tops you used and the size of the key, quite a large bang could be produced. Nowadays, I suspect something similar can be bought to produce the same effect, but without the fun or inventiveness of producing one.

Two-ball was another game played by those lucky enough to own two cheap tennis balls. This was mainly played by girls, who would bounce the balls on a wall and catch them in rotation with one hand. Another girls' game was what I can only call multiple skipping. This was where a very long piece of rope was swung by two girls who chanted a rhyme, while several other girls jumped in and out of the swinging rope quite skilfully.

Mill Street Memories

The following interviews are a small selection from the many recorded during the course of the Project, and which now form an extraordinary oral history of Mill Street. For reasons of space, they have been précised in places.

'I believe to call it a slum was all wrong! It was a neighbourhood of ordinary people, growing up together, living together, joining together, and that was what it was all about.'

Memories of a nonagenarian from Dorchester – Ivy Gale

One day the phone rang and a lady's voice said …

I am 97 and am worried that I am going to die without telling my life story. Would you consider writing it for me?

On occasions when researching or writing a book, one has a really lucky break, and this was mine. Ivy explained:

Our cottages were one room up and one room down. In the cottages at each end lived two ladies; however, our centre cottage was somewhat more crowded. I was the middle one of seven sisters, two of whom died. We all lived in the one room downstairs, then at night we all slept in the one room upstairs, us girls all in one bed, three across the top of the bed, two across the bottom. We continued these sleeping arrangements until two of the girls reached puberty and started their periods, at which time the girls were moved out, one to stay with Granny and the other to stay with Dad's sister. The cottages we lived in were served by one outside tap and one outside toilet between the three cottages.

At the time of interview in January 2014, Ivy was the last surviving of the children. At the beginning of her life she lived in Standfast Road, which ran along what is now Kings Road, opposite the Methodist Chapel.

The houses faced the bank of St George's graveyard. Here a great number of my family were buried. They are all up one side of the path. The caretaker at the cemetery at the time was Mr Walton.

Ivy's grandmother was a Voss and lived in Holloway Road; her other grandparents, the Gales, lived in Cokers Frome. As we will hear later, this part of her extended family became a very important lifeline.

Jane, my mother, managed all cooking in the one downstairs room, heating pots over an open fire. (They had no range or Aga.) Once a week a long bath was brought in from the yard, kettles and pots were boiled and the whole family bathed in turn.

A typical shepherd's hut, home for weeks on end.

My father John was a steam-roller driver for Eddisons, a big company based in Wareham Road, Fordington, so he worked away a lot. He would tow a shepherd's-type hut behind his machine in which to spend the night. Every few weeks I would travel with my Mum Jane to take Dad clean clothes. I was a Dad's girl really.

Eddison Steam Rolling Company had contracts to mend and build roads all over Dorset. John's machine had a device fitted to the side to rip up the old road surface. New material was then put down and rolled in.

Unfortunately, when I was quite young my father had a bad accident. He was in hospital for a year. At this time he also developed a weak heart.

This, as we can imagine, put an enormous burden on Ivy's mother Jane, as her father never really worked again. In those days there was no social security, you were on your own. Jane took in washing and worked at the Union (the Workhouse) to make ends meet, though Ivy never went hungry. *'We never ate dry bread, there was always something to put on it,'* Ivy stressed. We can see from this that Jane was a good manager and very hard worker. However, they were all fortunate to have a wider family to lean on.

> *On a Friday I would go down to Eddisons with my little trolley to meet the carrier and he would bring a sack of vegetables from Granny and Granddad Gale. These vegetables would get us through the week. Always sewn into the top corner of the bag would be a six-penny piece, a huge help in those days.*
>
> *Once a week my sister and I would visit the Moule Institute where the ladies of the church would hand us two long loaves of bread. We couldn't have managed without the ladies of the church.*

This fact is interesting as John was a Salvationist, very strict, who never smoked or drank. Jane, who was actually Welsh, was a Methodist and refused to change to the Salvation Army. It is clear that none of this stood in the way of the help being given by the Church at the Moule Institute (now sadly demolished).

Boys reading, possibly in the Moule Institute Reading Room. I wonder how many of them could actually read!

From a very early age Ivy discovered that, like her mother, she had a voice.

> *At the age of 5 I was sitting on the stage at the Corn Exchange with a basket of flowers singing 'Will you buy my pretty flowers?' I have always had a voice and sang in choirs, but now my voice is gone, I can't sing any more.*

Despite living in abject poverty, Ivy's mother was intent that they should all have clean clothes and a starched piny. When Ivy was four, she and her sisters were fishing with a jam jar by the mill when she was pushed over by a bigger boy and floated off down the river, supported by the air trapped under her starched piny. The current was quite fast and Ivy was carried along until spotted by a sharp-eyed woman from the 'Big House' on the corner, who pulled her out before she was swept off through the hatches. Ivy cannot remember this, but the story was related to her by her parents.

I attended St George's Infants School at the top of High Street from the age of three. Sometimes I had a problem as I couldn't pull my knickers up properly or tie up my boots. So occasionally I would have to run off down Holloway Road, knickers around my ankles, boots in my hand, to Granny Voss who sorted me out.

When aged 7, I moved on to the Gasworks School in Icen Way. When we needed coke, I would take my little trolley to school so that on the way home I could take a sack of coke with me.

Times being so hard, nothing much would be expected at Christmas. However, we never went without, we each had a black stocking; this would contain an orange, apples, perhaps a pear that had

The old Gasworks School in Icen Way.

A Christmas party organised by the Mission – one of the few treats at Christmas.

been stored and fruit cake, etc. There was always a silver three-penny piece sewn into the top.

These, like much else, were supplied by the grandparents. This tradition still lives on in the family, continued first by Ivy and now her daughter.

During Ivy's school days many of the children suffered from diphtheria.

A number of the parents thought it came from using the "swimming baths" at Grey's Bridge, which were then closed. Basically, the baths were fed with river water and the cows were in the river upstream, probably a health hazard, which still existed when I was a child (at this time, however, the health scare was polio).

Young ladies having tea (with Lily Gale, who suffered from polio and was in a wheelchair, and friends).

Ivy, along with many others, went down with diphtheria and was put into the Isolation Hospital in Herringston Road. These were old timber-built buildings with tin roofs. Ivy remembers it well.

The Isolation Hospital was totally overcrowded, the beds were side by side with hardly any room to move. I think I was about ten at the time. In my childhood (in the 1940s) these buildings had become the TB Isolation Hospital.

By the age of eight Ivy was busy doing lots of jobs for her mother.

Twice a week I would take my little cart loaded with clean washing up to Max Gate for the Hardys. My two sisters, Nelly and Bessie, were at this time working for Thomas Hardy, one as a chambermaid, the other in the kitchen. Thomas Hardy would often see me as I walked through the garden with my little cart, but never once spoke or gave me a smile of recognition. Mrs Hardy, however, always made a fuss of me and would give me a piece of fruit from the fruit bowl.

Life was hard for the two girls in service and days were long.

Mr Hardy was prone to follow the chambermaids around and would often remove coal from the newly made-up fire. When it came to meal times, he controlled how much the staff could eat. The cook was not allowed to have the remaining joint. He would carve the staff a slice of meat each, then it was put away!

Then came that fateful day, 11 January 1928.

I was now aged 11 and arrived as usual with my little cart bearing the clean washing. As I approached the house my sister ran to meet me. 'You can't come round to the kitchen,' she said, 'you will have to come around the side. The old man has died and they are all in the kitchen with him'. Well, as it turned out, Thomas Hardy's heart was removed there and then, and put into an Oxo tin; from there it was transferred into a casket, supplied by the undertaker, and then taken to Stinsford Vicarage, until it was put into the grave. Once the Oxo tin was empty, Mrs Hardy made the gardener dig a deep hole in a far corner of the garden and bury the tin. I could still point out where the tin was buried. The cat never did eat his heart, that was a fallacy.

Once before, Ivy had been approached by the Hardy Society and asked about T.H.

I would not talk to them, as there was not too much good to be said about him, and I didn't think they were looking for bad news.

From my point of view I was not surprised by this comment as I was once introduced to his last housekeeper, whose only comment about him was 'Horrible man!' Having heard this from two totally different sources, one has to wonder if perhaps he was different with friends and acquaintances than he was to those who worked for him.

By the time Ivy was in her teens the Gales had moved to Fordington Hill, near the builder's yard.

With my sister, I used to go out to dances. There were two rules: we had to be back home by 9 o'clock and we must not dance with soldiers. The second rule, of course, we often broke as we loved dancing with soldiers. One drawback to this was that soldiers wore white belts and the white came off onto our dresses while dancing close! So, a routine developed. Beforehand, we would stand outside the nearby shop and rub the white off our dresses and inspect each other before entering the house.

John, like many fathers, had a soft spot for the girls and would often overlook lateness.

As our house was built up against the builder's yard it made it possible to get over the low wall, onto the lid of the water butt and in through our bedroom window.

Ivy said her mother would quite often say:

'Those girls are late again, John.' Good old Dad having heard us creep in would say, 'Oh no, Jane, they are upstairs in bed'.

After a while, however, John decided this had to stop. Unknown to the girls, he removed the lid from the water butt. Grinning, Ivy went on to say:

We arrived home and made our usual entrance; however, as I stepped over the wall I went deep into the water, there being no lid on the butt! I had no choice but to wring out my clothes as best I could and hide them under other clothes ready for the wash.

Next morning their father said, *'Lot of noise out the back last night!'* Ivy replied quick as a flash, *'That must have been old Tom, the cat, again.'*

The big day in St George's Church. (Courtesy of Ivy Gale.)

However, they knew the game was up!

Ivy married a 20-year-old soldier, William Hain, from Yeovil, when she was 18 and a half. However, her hard life was not over.

My husband was in Bomb Disposal and was damaged by shrapnel in his neck. At the same time I was a sergeant driving a lorry which carried a barrage balloon. I had my 21st birthday at this time but I didn't really know I was 21 until a card arrived from my mother. Despite my husband's injuries, he worked for many years as a bus driver until he was unable to work due to his health. He eventually went blind and I had to nurse him. He lived until he was ninety but I continued to nurse him at home, for many years. Finally, he went into hospital for the last year of his life as I was not allowed to have him home. This made me very sad as they didn't think I could look after him anymore, but I so wanted to.

None of the women like Ivy received medals for their war-time service. However, when Ivy was 95 she was presented with a Voluntary Service Medal; the vast majority of the other ladies had probably passed away by then.

Ivy's Voluntary Service Medal. (Courtesy of Ivy Gale.)

Interview with Peggy Peplow, born in 1931 into a family of 16 children

When I was three, I moved to 3 Hardy Avenue, Dorchester, until I was 23 years old and got married. I was married in St George's Church, Fordington. I have very fond memories of growing up in Mill Street. At 3 years old I went to Fordington Infants School; we had a raffia mat, as we always had to sleep in the afternoon. We were given ½ a pint of milk a day.

Their mother encouraged them all to read. When Peggy went to school she can only remember learning Reading, Writing and Arithmetic.

I went to all girls schools until I was 11 years old, but then they built a new school and I was there until I was 14.
I went to work at Woolworths, 5½ days a week. On Sundays I worked as a waitress up Wessex Guest House. Growing up in Mill Street we had plenty of friends, played together, no trouble. We had to go to Chapel twice a day on Sunday, all in our best clothes which were just for Sunday school.

Sunday School group outside the Mission.

When asked about outings and her father having time off work, she replied:

No, we only went to the seaside, only there. Yes, well he had time off but he ... we were all the same, there wasn't anybody going on trips, we couldn't afford it. We went to Weymouth on outings quite a lot. We had tea at the Salvation Army Hall.

On Tuesday we went to Christian Endeavour – girls made shopping baskets, we would have to collect the tops of milk bottles, they had a little hole in the middle of them. We would put raffia round them. The boys made things like woodwork.

We as a family were poor, but nearly all the people living there were not jealous of anyone. We were there for one another.

You said your mother never went out to work, just your father?

Yes, well then he was a builder and if, like, they built Marks & Spencer, he would help there; do you know what I mean? They were more or less odd-job men then.

One of my Dad's jobs was working in the cattle market, putting the lambs in their pens and the pigs in theirs for when they came for auction. There was always a market day on a Wednesday and Saturday at Dorchester. He had to wash and milk the cows for auction and the milk he got was his, so he had a big urn and another two men would carry it home because the milk was all Dad's; me and my brothers and sisters would take it in turns to fill a jug up with milk and take it to the neighbours and they would give us a penny for it, for more pocket money.

We also made cheese and butter; I am one of eight brothers and seven sisters. Four died very young. I remember when my Mum had a baby boy, Miss Vincent and the headmistress would always come and see my mum and the new baby, bring a large tin of biscuits.

Baby and toddler group, with Miss Godbehear, who lived at 15 South Walks – 'a saintly person'. She was one of the voluntary workers and was invited to become a permanent social worker for the Mission.

Mum had two sets of twins, one born on 14 February 1935 and the other April 1936. Four children in 14 months. One of the twins had a very bad skin condition only a couple of weeks old, she went into Dorchester County Hospital, they would not let her come home, instead they put her in Maiden Castle, she did not come ever again to live with us. We saw her every day as she went to the same school as us. Mum and Dad tried very, very hard to try to get her back home to live with us, but no one would listen. When she was 9 years old, they moved her all the way to Liverpool in a convent. The council gave us money to go to Liverpool on the train, we had to get bed and breakfast to bring her home for a holiday, and I always went with Mum to get her. They kept her in that convent until she was 20 years old and then let her out into the big wide world. She did get married and have a son. I love her very much.

I was the eldest of the girls so had to help Mum a lot. I had every Monday off school as it was her busiest day, but then every day was hard for her but I never heard her moan. We always had three meals a day and it was good food.

We grew our own veg and we had hens. Dad used to get out a trap for rabbits, Mum made a lovely rabbit pie. One of us would go to the Bakery and if they had any stale bread, which they always had, she would make lovely bread pudding and cakes. It was quite hard during the war times as everything was on ration. Her chocolate cake – other kids used to love her cakes too. I loved the suet pudding with treacle running down the sides.

This was the early 1940s and the country was on the brink of war. So what else was happening at this time?

I was 8 years old and home from chapel on a Sunday morning. I heard on the radio as it was a sunny day and people always had their doors and windows open that we were at war with Germany. It was 3 September and the Prime Minister, Mr Chamberlain, he said that when we heard this sound it was a siren to warn us that it was an air raid and we had to take shelter. Mrs White put her arms around me as I was so frightened.

When the American soldiers came in 1942 to Dorchester they came in large convoys. I did not know what racial meant until they were segregated – whether white or black they all went to war together and a lot of them got killed. When they got settled there used to be an MP at the top of Kings Road on duty. He would ask us kids if we would ask our mothers if they could make them a sandwich, which they did. They always gave us money, more pocket money!

The County Council put two big concrete posts at the bottom of Hardy Avenue road end to stop the jeeps going through. My younger brother, he was to get the soldiers' food, etc. from one of the four shops, two in Mill Street and two in Holloway Road. They brought him about to get the supplies.

When I was in my teens, we had plenty of British soldiers; I should know, I married one! We girls were asked if we would go to the Army training hall at the Barracks once a month. They would put records on and we would partner a soldier and we all learnt to dance. We had lemonade and biscuits; it was great growing up in Mill Street.

You said your mother was born in Mill Street, so you're all Mill Street stock? And that when you moved to Hardy Avenue you had quite a big house.

We had a three-bedroom house, quite new. It's the houses that are still there now. You then had a big hall, a scullery and then the bathroom, well the kitchen and scullery and three big bedrooms because you could get double beds in them, and Mum and Dad had the smallest room. The copper was in the bathroom, it was for water to give us baths once a week, to do the washing and cooking. They put the puddings in it. We had a big garden, plenty of room to play. When they used to chop down trees at Bluebell Copse, all the kids would get anything like an old pram or wheelbarrow and go to collect the logs. We slept four in a bed, two top and two bottom. It was fun. They were really large bedrooms.

Times were hard, but, if you know what I mean, I wouldn't say I was unhappy. It was lovely, it really was. It was only when the last six was born, they were a lot better off because we all went out to work. I worked on a Sunday, I gave my mum that money to help her and we all had jobs to do, like the boys used to chop sticks and light the fire and light the range with it. She had to pay sixpence or maybe threepence to a doctor, so you couldn't have free medicine; you never had any family allowance.

Making do – a hard life in Mill Street during the 1940s

The names of those in this story have been removed, given some of the content and as relatives are still alive.

I was born on 23 December 1940 and I started my life in Mill Street. We took my Mum's name, different from my Dad's. Most people didn't have a lot but I would say we were one of the poorest because of Dad's drinking! I was born with an illness and couldn't walk until the age of 18 months so Mum would have to take me to the hospital. We were a family of five children, three girls and two boys. I was the middle child. Mum had twin girls at the age of 42; only one lived, she slept in a large drawer. There were two bedrooms, one for Mum and Dad and ours was two beds in the other room – one bed for the two boys, the other for us two girls – only army coats were on the bed. We didn't have wardrobes, no posh cloths if we had, to put in them.

Mum worked very, very hard at Judge Jeffrey's washing up. Dad drank so there was no money, we had to go to jumble sales for our clothes and get some from the tally man. There was a lovely lady who tried to help us out with different things. One day I had a pair of square-toed shoes, they were really lovely, I thought, and they were like new, but they hurt my feet so badly. I didn't complain because I knew that I couldn't have another pair, so I crippled about and had to have them. Every Easter, Mum would buy us a new dress and we would have white socks. My pleasures were taking the cat in an old pram with no shade which Mum had taken off, I had no dolls. My favourite thing was picking up cigarette packets, cutting them into squares and using them as my cards.

Five stones was another game we played, also Hopscotch. We sometimes picked flowers – bunched them up and sold them for a penny. Guy Fawkes was absolutely great, we had a few coppers then. My step brother was in the Navy; he would come home quite often with food and goodies, oh how we loved those days and how we loved him. Mum would make toffee apples with him and everyone would enjoy them.

Our lovely neighbour sometimes helped Mum out by giving her half a meat pie, etc. We never complained as we didn't know any different. Christmas was a chicken, pork or beef, given by our neighbour as he worked on a meat lorry. Mum made rabbit stew which we all enjoyed and we got the veg from the stalls (still in same place). Broken biscuits from Woolworths, cakes from the Wessex as we knew the girl – that was a real luxury. Our Christmas present was an old sock with an apple, orange and some nuts. I remember the Dandy and the Beano, but they were not new. Mum used to sing wonderful songs and tell us about her life – how I used to love to listen. My aunt used to come and we had such good times with them. We would go up to the Exhibition (pub in London Road) and stay outside, quiet we hoped, to get a drink or a packet of crisps if we were lucky.

A bath once a week, in a tin bath in front of the fire. The one that was lucky was the first one in, but after about five children having a bath you

Ladies dressed in Sunday best inside the Mission Hall. Clothes were boiled in a copper and very white and Monday was wash day (no bonfires allowed by local law).

didn't get much joy out of that. The toilet was down the garden, we cut up squares of newspaper and tied them with string for toilet rolls. Mum had a stone copper in the back room for washing and a cooker with the bottom out.

My elder sister was our rock. She would take us to Weymouth or the café where we would have soup, etc. She would clean, darn and keep the house clean. She didn't have a child's life, but never complained because it wasn't Mum's fault. Christian Endeavour was great because we had a sandwich and a drink once a week. We went to the Mill Street Mission once a week on Sunday and Mrs Clark was really good to us.

Mum would send my sister or me up to Sophie's shop to get five woodbines, her only pleasure. She had holes in the soles of an old pair of plimsolls and would put cardboard in them to cover them up.

Or going to get crab apples that would make your tummy hurt. One day I didn't feel very well, was sat on the pot, my brother was home and told Mum to get the doctor. I was taken to the isolation hospital in Chickerell, had all my clothes burnt, which wasn't much, and stayed in the room on

We all used to go swimming in the swimming baths (the River Frome at Grey's Bridge). We would jump in – such a happy time.

my own. I thought I had done something wrong and was crying because nobody could explain to me why I was there and Mum just didn't have the time or the money to come and see me very often. I sang 'My Bonny Lies Over the Ocean' to a blind man who was in the next room. He used to say 'Go on, sing me another one'.

Sometimes Mum used to tear a page out of the back of a book and break a pencil in half for us to write with.

I can never remember my father having a conversation with any of us. He ruled Mum and he ruled us all. He would come home, have his own chair right in front of the fire, have the best of the meal and be waited on hand, foot and finger, and then each evening off down the pub. Very nice to everyone down the pub, would treat them really well, but never had any money for Mum or my brothers and sisters.

Also now I feel, many years later, that it does make you a better person. I can see now two sides of the coin, I can see when people are really poor and I can see when you do get a bit better off. I never take things for granted. I had a friend who was an only child who lived in Hardy's Avenue. She had wonderful clothes from America. I used to dream and think, if only I could have something like her, but I knew that nice clothes were not on our list.

When Mum had the twins, one of which died, she had to stay in hospital for a long while, so we had to go to a neighbour for about 6 weeks. I used to pine inwardly for Mum and couldn't wait to go back to her. Even though life was hard at Mill Street, you would never say out loud how you really felt, for fear of upsetting Mum. All children were seen but not heard and if you were invited into somebody's house you always waited at the door to be asked in.

Sometimes we would go to bed just a little bit hungry, but we couldn't do anything about that. We had bread and milk for breakfast, maybe now and again we would have mashed potato, beans and sausages. My elder sister was a wonderful cook when Mum couldn't do it.

I remember once I wanted my hair cut. Mum couldn't afford to have it done, so my brother said he would cut it, but what I forgot was that he had been drinking so wasn't really capable of cutting it. However, when he had finished I looked in the broken mirror and cried and cried. I had been cropped, I had never seen anything like it! Mum said, 'I'm sorry, my love, but you kept on and on and that's the way it has become'. I don't know how I got to school but I think many people laughed at me for a long time because they thought I looked so funny.

One thing Mum tried to keep up was bringing us home little treats, maybe a packet of sweets. She would share them between us, five each I think. We all thought we were lucky but I had a habit of keeping mine, I don't know why. I wasn't a goody goody, but I could see my younger sister looking at me and thinking 'Oh, you're 5 years older than me'. Maybe I would give her one, maybe I would give her two, I can't really remember, but I know I would give her something.

We all doted on my young sister, what with her being so small at birth and the last child, thank God. We just didn't have any room for any more, or any money. I can't remember where my brother slept when he was on leave – my sister may know.

Manners were always very strict, we never ever forgot to say please or thank you or even sorry, and even today I overdo the pleases and thanks.

My brother younger than me by 15 months was eating a jam sandwich once, stood on a windowsill. He was bitten by a wasp, I think his tongue swelled up, but like many many things he wouldn't do anything about it.

He was okay after a while. Another time I remember he went fishing with some lads. He couldn't have been much more than 6 years old, but as he was running across Grey's Bridge, he got run over by a car. They took him to hospital but I can't remember how. Then when the nurse undid his shirt a fish fell out. She screamed and screamed and the thing was it was written in the paper about it because afterwards it was so funny, plus my brother loved all the fuss and presents – who wouldn't, living in Mill Street!

One Christmas I was given a pair of gloves and some sweets from an uncle who belonged to my sister's friend. Oh how I loved those gloves and those sweets, it really made my Christmas and I think the rest of us.

We had some lovely neighbours and friends, some who lived in Hardy's Avenue. One family had 12 children living, but I think they actually had 18, I'm not sure though. Another family were lovely, their father always worked, so they were really lucky. I can remember the Ottons, the Whites, Blackwells, Symes and Dufalls, they all lived in Mill Street or thereabouts.

Mum had some money left her by her family before she met Dad. Mum came from quite a well-off family, but it didn't take Dad long to get rid of it. He took up a van and did some fish hawking and most days spent time in the pub. Mum couldn't do anything about it, so nearly all the money went, which was quite a lot in those days. She could have bought two houses in London Road but didn't.

Sometimes I laugh about these things in Mill Street, how we actually had to survive, but if we didn't laugh where would we be? One day, I remember my older sister having to take some rags up to Dad's cousin, but I think Mum being Mum, to try and get more money, put a brick in with the cloths, but I'm not too sure, and he gave us extra money anyway which really did help out. He didn't say a word because he was frightened of Dad like many, many people were. Dad was a bully!

We were sometimes allowed to go to the Palace cinema on a Saturday morning – who would make sure we went? My big sister, of course, she always seemed to be busy shopping and doing things, washing, cleaning floors and doing everything she could. She hardly ever went out. If she went out it would be to go to the cinema on a Saturday night, but bless her one evening she was running late. She ran up Mill Street, along the river path and knocked her hand on the rail, and her precious sixpence dropped in the river. Even to this day I still think about that sixpence and try to find it – ha ha. So she couldn't go after all, she had to come back. Bless her heart, she made our lives so much more comfortable.

Mum's mother and father owned a farm, so we should have been comfortable. We didn't know if Mum and Dad were married. My Grandfather died just after the First World War, so we never saw him, Mum was about 14. Her mother died when I was four or five; by then she had taken to drink so she didn't leave the amount of money she could have done, but still left them all a lot of money because of their lifestyle. They were so well off when Mum was a child that they used to have their coats made in Genges, the large store on the corner of Trinity Street and High West Street. So she had gone a long way from having coats made in Genges to wearing plimsolls with cardboard covering up the holes in the soles.

Mum had been married before and had one son, but we never knew him till much later. Dad was married before and had five children. When his wife left him the children had to go into care. Our step-brother we got to know very well, we liked him. Well, we liked them all, when we got to know them and we were older and they got married.

Dad was a big burly sort of man, he was a strong man and a fighter. He used to go to fairs and they had the Boxing Booth; he used to do the boxing, he won quite a lot, he was really strong.

We would do the shopping. Mum would leave one and three pence on the mantelpiece to do the shopping, and this was the list:

Three penn'th of mixed veg
Three penn'th picked fruit
Yesterday's cakes
Bread
Broken biscuits

When I used to go to Woolworths to get the broken biscuits, I used to say 'please can you pick out the chocolate ones', not realising it was a cheek or wrong in any way, I just thought it was part of the grocery list. I used to love it if we went to the greengrocers and there was a mushroom box there, because I used to feel so posh to be carrying this box, they were the ones with the handle over the top. I loved these boxes, they were so much better than the brown paper bags with string handles that were always breaking.

Sunday was a special day. Sometimes Mum would give a shilling to go up to the Wessex, that was the tearooms. There were two waitresses there; one of them we knew well and we used to get her to serve us because we would ask for a shilling's worth of cakes – the cakes were four pence each so there should only be three cakes, but when our friend served us we would get a bag of cakes. We lived in fear of the other waitress coming to serve us, we couldn't very well say we want our friend to serve us. So we had to wait until our friend was in the room, because they also waited at tables as well as at the counter.

We had one trip a year with the Mill Street Mission, that was to Weymouth. We would feel sick with excitement. No other trips, as the train fare was eight

Outing from Dorchester West railway station c 1920: note the children's metal buckets and spades. There used to be separate men's and ladies' waiting rooms with a warm fire inside.

pence; to get the eight pence was something. Everything was a luxury – everything.

I remember the American soldiers. They were billeted here with anyone who had a spare room, but we didn't, obviously. Dad would go to the pub most nights. He was so generous to everybody,

Beach outing.

he would bring a couple home and Mum would give them supper, whatever we had, which as you know was very little. They were so generous; the next day they would come round with butter and all sorts for Mum because they knew that what she had given them was all she had and they were grateful. My brother was only little and he used to grab hold their trousers; they were really keen on having their cloths immaculate, the creases in their trousers … he would grab their legs and ask for gum and they would give him some to get him away from them, I suppose. They used to put on some good parties, I remember going to the parties. Some were billeted around North Square, there were some around there.

I left school when I was 15. There were plenty of jobs around and you could get a different one every week, not that I left the one I had, I just loved getting jobs, they were really, really easy. I worked for the Wessex Hotel at the Top o' Town and I was supposed to be a waitress but I also did all their cleaning and everything. I had a thing about cleaning and she used to let me do all their private quarters in the winter when they were quiet, just to keep me.

A glimpse into the life of the younger sister, the surviving twin

I left school at 14. I was allowed to then as I was 15 in December. I worked in Genges, there were plenty of jobs about and there was no problem at all. Really we needed to get a job to help Mum. My brothers all got jobs and gave Mum some rent, we all did.

Even when I went away to work, I was in living on a farm, for a Brigadier's little boy, and I sent money home then and so did my brother from the Merchant Navy. We definitely, definitely would never be without work and would never, ever fail to give Mum our keep – ever, none of us, would we? We all thought the world of her, we would all give her our lives, let alone anything else.

My first wage was £1, 5s (£1.25p) and I had tips. I had dinner at dinner time, so only went home for tea, which was a great help to Mum. I gave Mum 15 shillings, so I was left with 10 shillings. We didn't stop for breakfast or anything, and on our day off we used to help with the cleaning. We would clean windows or do the ironing, and on a Sunday morning I would clean the bedrooms when I was at home. So we still helped Mum out. Mum was still working, she had worked all her life, she worked really hard.

As well as the bath house, a laundry room was provided by the Mission.

It seems that most of the men in Mill Street worked, I don't remember any men being at home, and they must have been out doing something. I also don't remember any family being as poor as us. I remember the man next door – he always worked, his wife had a fur coat and a new three-piece suite. Upstairs they had a rocking horse, huge it was and we were allowed to go on it!

Everyone down there worked or they would work; even if they went out in the evenings, their wives weren't as bad off as Mum. I don't think the other men drank as much as Dad. He did a bit of fish hawking, but he didn't do it for long, I don't know why, it was just his way.

The gas lights in Mill Street were gas mantles, but we never had a globe, in all the years we lived there, we never had a globe and he used to come in drunk, and every week regularly, we would get the mantles ready to put out because they were so fragile, you can't breathe on them, can you The rest of the rooms we had candles; it was just in the one room that we had a gas mantle.

Dad would come home drunk every night. This was good because we didn't want him to come home anyway, life was so much better when he wasn't there. He wouldn't dream of chopping wood, Mum did everything, lit the fires, chopped the wood, everything. When Mum was ill and couldn't do it, we had to do it, it still had to be done.

We were on the council waiting list for 19 years, but he wouldn't accept a council house because the rent at Mill Street was eight shillings and four pence a week, but the council house when we eventually moved was nineteen shillings and seven pence. I don't think he was paying it, that's why Mum was working so hard, but he still wouldn't move, he was quite content with his life in Mill Street, why wouldn't he be? Not only that, he didn't do anything different when we moved, it didn't make any difference to him at all. His lifestyle wasn't any different whatsoever.

I think we had a rent man call. I know the tally man called, because I got into trouble one day because Mum didn't have any money for the Pat Man, we called him. You paid the tally man a shilling a week or something for any bits you had bought like clothes. He came one day and Mum didn't have any money to give him so she went into the back house, whilst in the front room Dad's father who was an antique dealer had a beautiful big sideboard with a mirror on top. So I went to the door as a child to say to the man that Mum was out; sadly he could see Mum's reflection in the mirror. He shouted out 'Don't teach your children to tell lies', that taught me! I have never since told a lie, I couldn't lie even if you begged me to, and I was so frightened.

The milkman was Norman's. They used to deliver with a push bike and two cans one on each handle with a dipper, you had to have your jug to put it in, that was another novelty down there.

Post? I never remember having any post, I don't remember a letter at all, and I don't think we had a letter box – did anyone? We didn't have telephones or anything. Sometimes I wonder if we had a front door, but I know we did, but it didn't have a letter box, it opened straight off the street, I remember scrubbing the front step.

We had an allotment. My brother made a shed out there when he was a bit older, and he lined the shed with sacking, made a lovely shed, we used to go there, and it was lovely. We had a candle in there and the candle burnt the shed, the shed went up in flames, everyone was panicking beyond a joke because the Blackwells had a thatched roof, and they were worried to death

Typical tumbled-down cottage.

because the sparks and everything was flying. Fortunately a man came out with a hose which he put on the outside tap and doused the flames. But we were in big trouble!

I don't remember anyone having chickens or pigs to help supplement their food, but some may have. We had enough trouble feeding ourselves! We did have a ferret, I put my hand in the cage and got bitten and it just would not let go, I've still got the scar. Anyway, when I finally got my finger out I was crying, then Dad came along and clipped me around the ear for putting my finger in.

It was always better not to say anything, just bleed to death. You didn't say anything because poor old Mum, she didn't have the time ...Like I say, I went to the jumble sale, Mum never came because she had to be in when the Old Man came home. She would give me a shilling and ask me to get stuff at the jumble sale, but she would have really liked to have come, it would have been an hour out for her, but no, she never came to a jumble sale. She never went anywhere, ever, only to work. There were never ever any holidays.

She did come on the Sunday School outing because when we got to Weymouth it was this big church near Alexandra Gardens, I think it's a Baptist church, I'm not sure. We could go all day on the beach with all the families, but at tea time we would go in there as part of our treat. The mothers had to pay one shilling and three pence to pay for their tea, but I remember Mr Oates, he was one of the Sunday School teachers. He let Mum come in for free, so she had an extra one and three pence.

Tea with the Sunday School teacher Mr Oates.

All aboard for a Sunday School outing (1920s).

So yes, there were some kind people in Mill Street; trouble was they didn't have a lot themselves. I remember they made a bread pudding between them, they made it in a big roasting tin, the big kind you roast your meat in. One of the neighbours did most of it, but they still shared it out – things like that people did to help you. One lady, Mrs Baskett, had lots of children and she used to make the most delicious chocolate cake. When I used to call round for her daughter she would sometimes cut me off a tiny bit, even with all those children, and that was the most wonderful chocolate cake, it was lovely.

People were all marvellous. If anybody ever had anything, they wouldn't see you go without; trouble was they often didn't have anything themselves. I don't think anybody, and I'm not just saying this, but I really don't think there was anybody worse off than us, but we didn't take any notice, it didn't hurt us, not at all; in fact, like my sister said earlier, it made us what we are today.

The neighbours were friendly and all that, even if they were better off than us. I mean, you wouldn't get it today, we know, but then they would really, really help you. They didn't look down on you, I mean you might get a few that would look down on you, but on the whole they were wonderful people, wonderful.

You never, ever locked your door, not day or night, the door was never locked. If I went home from school in the day time, if my brother had messed his trousers and I was sent home to get a clean pair, I knew I would be able to get in. Mum had gone to work, the house was empty and I just went in.

Mum was house proud, outstandingly so. She washed up and swept up after every meal. We didn't have much, it might have been darned up to the hilt and Mum couldn't see very well; they had one pair of glasses and when Dad went out Mum could have the glasses, otherwise Dad would have them for reading the paper, he could always afford that. The radio was Radio Relay; it was plugged in, nothing was a luxury to him. Then poor Mum would have to sew with a darning needle because she couldn't see very well. Dad had his drinking pals living down the other end, there was always money for the pub.

There was a lady lived the other side of the alleyway. She was marvellous. If Mum had a confinement at home she would act as midwife. Down the alleyway was an old man who lived on his own and he would let us go in there in the evenings. We would go in because he always had a roaring fire, also we would be out of the house, so we would go in there whenever we could. He would have all the kids around the fire, he didn't mind what we did. I think we were all just good company for him. Next door to him was a lady who lived on her own, a bit reserved, but when it was harvest festival, she had a beautiful flower garden, she would let us do a big bunch of flowers for three pence to take to the harvest festival, because obviously there wasn't any food to take; in fact we could have done with some of it, couldn't we!

The Mission Hall dressed up for harvest.

Then there was several houses with people in around the alley, then a derelict one on the corner. Mum's cousin was in one of the houses down there, you just wouldn't believe how many houses were put in there; 20, 21, 24 and 25 were occupied, 22 and 23 were down.

We celebrated the Queen's Coronation I remember, had a street party. That meal must have been one of the best we ever had. It was marvellous; they all got together and did it. That was down outside the Mill Street Mission, where they put the tables out, there was a bit of a car park out in front.

Our meals were usually bread and milk for breakfast, then we would go to school at St George's and over the Moule Institute for our dinner which was school dinners and they were absolutely brilliant, we used to get really excited when we had school dinners. Then we would go home for tea which consisted of a cake each, and bread, butter and jam, that was our tea and supper. Sometimes Mum used to send me up to Polkes to get a couple of Oxo's, three candles and her five cigarettes. We used to have Oxo's for supper with bread and that was very nice as well, that was our meals. When I got old enough, on a Saturday when Mum was working I used to go up the fish shop and get chips for the kids. Then when I got a bit older than that, I used to cook a meal for the children every Saturday – sausages, mashed potato and onion gravy.

If Mum was going to – God love her, I never saw her eat a cooked meal – but if she did have something to eat it was either a piece of crust with a little bit of

Coronation Tea Party, 4 June 1953. One thing they did well were street parties. Identified in the picture are David Holden, Terry White, Colin Baskett, one of the Harrison boys, Alan Congdon, Graham Loader and Marion Otton, with Mrs McCaughey (lady standing in front of the group).

butter on it and a bit of cheese; she used to sit and eat that and she was really sweet and I used to think, oh if only I could have a bit of your crusts Mum. She was so good really, I used to love watching her eat it, she ate it with relish, when she hadn't anything else to eat, she used to go without for us children.

Dad never ever ate margarine, always butter! Not even in the war with ration books, he always had the butter. Of course there was seven of us, so at 2 oz butter per person per week it wasn't too bad, and then there was margarine. All the food was on ration.

We started to go up to Liptons (one of the grocery stores in Dorchester) for our shopping, and the man in Liptons, the manager, I can see him now, a little man. We used to go up Top o' Town fish shop; the lady was Mum's cousin, she worked serving the fish and chips. You could have a penn'th of scrumps, that was the bits of batter that had fallen off the main of the fish, that was nice. Now I can't even eat batter. To this day I hate batter! So does my sister. I wonder why? It makes me feel really ill.

Mum would never answer Dad back, she wouldn't dare. This is why it was wrong of him, she was so inoffensive, she would do anything for him, anything to put things right and to keep it right for him. So there was no need. Some of my brothers stood up for Mum when they were big enough; he stopped then because the boys were bigger. He was such a bully! Not many people would stand up to him.

I was only 13 when I left Mill Street, so the others were that much younger. My brother was 15 and had gone into the Merchant Navy by then.

I really think that's about it.

Interview with Frank Voss

How and when did your family come to the area?

My father's family go back probably 250 years. He was born in No. 8 Pound Lane in 1910 and it was quite a big family, the Voss's, but as happened quite a lot was illegitimate, so he kept his mother's name of Voss, they didn't know who the father was. They moved into Holloway Road, I think there was a big house there; about 12 kids grew up in there. He went to school, like we all did, to Fordington and then Grey School Passage, and then was thrown out at 14 and had to go and find his own living, which he went gardening for Major Markham. Then he joined the army as soon as he could and that was his life up until after the war.

Just before the war he met my mother; she came from Bridport and she came to Dorchester then to live. During the war she followed him around; he was a gunnery instructor in Topsham in Exeter. He was an RSM but he had to come out after the war as he had perforated ear drums and that's not good being a gunner. He came back to Dorchester and managed to get a little house at the bottom of Holloway Road, two up two down, no bathroom – outside toilet. I was born in 1945 at my gran's house in Bridport because my mother went there because the men were busy at the end of the war. We came back to Dorchester in 1946. I went to St George's Infants. In 1955 we moved from there to Kings Road, where I stayed until I got married in 1964. We lived at No. 40 Holloway Road and moved to No. 20 Kings Road (just opposite the Mill); we lived at the second one up, Mrs Carol Lake on the end, the Carts and the Terns.

What were the schools like then?

I didn't like Fordington. The first year was alright. I remember Mrs King, she made us all lie down after dinner and have a sleep. I didn't like warm milk, when they used to warm the milk up; freezing cold I could drink a pint easily, warm milk I hated. If it had coffee in then OK, but we didn't have coffee then.

The middle teacher Miss Palmer, I hated her. Mrs Parsons, I think she was trained in Nazi Germany to be a teacher. We just wanted to get out as quickly as we could to play with our mates. They didn't really teach us anything, or not me anyway, and I know a few other people who learned less than that.

The teachers at the Infants School, Mr Treweller at Colliton Street Boys School, he was nice but he left after my first proper year. Then we had a Mr Kersey but he was a bit stricter. Mr Treweller went to the new school down Damers Road. We had a Mr Westlake, Mr House and a Miss Minterne, she used to do the music, and I always remember the cook.

Apart from that, before I got there, it was still the Sunday School and the Sunday school was the only one which gave us a holiday, if you like, and that was only one day. My holiday when I was growing up was probably a weekend with my mum's family at Bridport – when I say the weekend, everybody worked Saturday dinnertime, so I'm talking the Saturday dinnertime about catching the bus and coming back Sunday night. It was either there or my father's mother who lived in Corfe Castle then, the train down to Wareham

The annual group photo outside the church in Weymouth – before or after the Marmite sandwiches and orangeade.

and the other one back to Corfe Castle and that was it. The Mill Street gave us that one day in Weymouth – brilliant, everybody loved it, and we went to the same place every year, Alexandra Gardens for our tea.

When we were at Boy's School you had Carey Camp. It was an odd week; you went on Monday morning and came back Friday afternoon. It was in tents in Wareham, away from your mother for the first time – that was when none of us combed our hair, and they made us have a wash. We never combed our hair; our mother's always did it for us.

Can we go back to the Colliton Street school a second? Was Mr Strickland there when you were there?

Yes, I'd forgotten Strickland, and I didn't like him very much. You took your 11+ at the end there, and I think there was no doubt that the Goulds were going to Grammar School, whether they were the thickest person in that school, they were going to Grammar school – you could have been the brightest. No, that is wrong, the brightest may have got in. If you had more sense than the Goulds and you come from Mill Street you didn't go to Hardye's.

I think we were discriminated against. I don't know if that was in a nasty way or whether they were just trying to say, you know, that your parents can't afford to send you to that school.

I'm not getting at the Goulds, it's not the boys' fault that their parents had money; they were going to Hardye's whichever way it was.

There were quite a few boys of your sort of age that went to Hardye's?

Oh yes. We had David Hallett, who I lived next door to when we moved round to Kings Road. Ray McCorkie went, as we know he went on to become a teacher.

I think the ordinary day-to-day boys and girls they were sort of excluded from it.

Yes, I know people who didn't go and went to Dorchester Modern, went in the Services and ended up as a chief technician on the trains. Even somebody like me, I went into building and when I retired I had more certificates than I wanted; I got my site manager bit, I was a health and safety inspector, an asbestos inspector, you know. I think, as my life went on, school changed; they didn't treat you as kids as you got older and went into education – 16, 17+

the teachers are treating you like adults and you learn more. We could never prove it, there was always talk that if you were in with Mr Hamilton, I think, the name of the headmaster of Hardye's, you were in. You can't prove it but that was the story all around the town.

Let's face it, they weren't interested in the boys with their asses hanging out of their trousers. It didn't matter really, as we had such a good education at the Modern School.

I'm not knocking Modern School; there were some teachers that I didn't like and some that I really did like. I didn't like Mr Griffin very much, the music teacher. Mr Jones was a good teacher – bit strict. Mr Dawes was alright. Bonfield should never have been allowed to teach children. He wouldn't get a job in school now, he taught woodwork and not very good at that. He put me off of woodwork. We had some nice teachers – David Downton, really nice chap. His younger brother Adrian Downton went to grammar school and went on to become a teacher. We had some good teachers and some bad ones.

At least we had some facilities there. Colliton Street was just disgraceful; it was a slum school, wasn't it, with open air toilets.

Yes, it was the best thing when it was shut down. Like you said, Modern School it was nice up there for people moving around. Yes, completely different. You weren't stuck with one teacher, how can one teacher teach you everything anyway? How can he teach maths and then English, art and geography, there's no way! Up there you went to Mrs so and so for English, somebody else for history and they was all good.

When I left there I went to Weymouth technical college for a year full time at Newstead Road. ... My father went and got me a job on Ricardo's (local building contractors), *but Ricardo said it was better if you go to Weymouth for a year; he wasn't paying me, mind, but I ended up staying on the same amount of time but the last year was down Weymouth. We did all the trades at that time, still maths and English down there as well; it was a step up again, they were treating you as an older person again. Don't forget I was only 15. In 4 years you went from being treated like a little boy at Colliton Street to down there being treated as a man. By the time I left I was old enough to join the services, you are a man in there, and there was no such thing as boys in there at that time.*

So, you went back to Ricardo when you'd finished there?

Men at work.

Yes, when I left there I went to Ricardo's on Fordington Green, a 5-year apprenticeship then, by the way, not the 2-year stuff now they're throwing out. I would say Ricardo's were the biggest firm in Dorchester, the Cakes were very close, you had Angels, but they were smaller; Ricardo's probably had 16–17 people there.

I was on Ricardo's when we knocked the last few houses down at Mill Street, the ones at the top before you went into Mill Street. The rest down the bottom by the chapel was gone, the flats were being built. At the top, Ricardo built two pairs of houses and one single one at the time. Charlie Mills lived in one of the semi-detached ones and Mrs Blackwell lived in the detached one which is now semi-detached. That's where we found an old rusty machine gun and we buried that under the patio of your house in Prince of Wales Road. All the wood was rotted away but it was the metal frame, I don't think it would ever be able to be fired again. We found a German helmet there which ended up at the Dorchester museum, not the Military one because it wasn't there; we found that in one of the out houses. You know they came back from the war and brought these things back.

I think all the people who lived down there, they were dirt poor, didn't have anything, but they all joined up in the First World War. So when you were growing up, were a lot of the soldiers coming back from the Second World War?

Well, I was too young to notice, I was born right at the end. I can remember people going off to do their national service. I remember my brother going away; he was an apprentice as well on Ricardo's, with a few others – 'Cheddar' Cheeseman, John and Teddy Brewer, they was all apprentices, so their national service was deferred until they finished their apprenticeship, but they had to go to night classes with the TA at the weekends. Then they had to go in. You didn't stop your apprenticeship, go in and then come out and carry on; you finished your apprenticeship first. I remember my brother going away to weekend camps with Cheddar and all them and coming back with bars of chocolate because they could get chocolate before it came off rationing here.

Have you ever been down the bunkers at Came Woods?

Yes, I expect I could find them if they're still there. They had a trap door and you go down. The iron beds were still there where they pulled them off the wall, no mattresses just the springs, but loads of women's underwear down there.

The army side of it, I can remember Poundbury Road with the sentry box, barracks and TA centre. Before you go over the bridge, there was a sentry box there with a boom (barrier) that came down and you stopped and they asked you blah, blah, blah, no you aren't coming down this way, yes you are, and you go on. Same going on down the Grove, there's another one there.

Because the Barracks in those days extended all the way down, right the way across Poundbury, didn't it? There were huts all the way across those houses.

All where those caravans are now, there were mostly tents there; I remember they had a miniature assault course down there with a swinging bridge and tunnels, where Travis Perkins is now. After they all moved out, the kids moved in, didn't we? We had the pleasure of smashing panes of glass like when everybody moved out of Mill Street, there weren't many panes of glass left. Worse thing is – it's a crime really – remember those Dorset clay pots you used to get, the dark and light brown things? Worth a bit of money now; I've got a few actually, the ones which were 6 inches high, probably worth £10 now, but when Mill Street moved out we put them up on the wall and took turns to throw stones at them to break them, that's what we used to do.

When they were all pulled down I remember that some of the boys your sort of age, bigger boys than us, they went through and got all the lead and everything out of it.

A bit older than me, it wasn't me, because I was stupid, I didn't realise how much it was worth; otherwise I would have joined in, but I didn't, I can honestly say. What I can remember is I lived in Kings Road then, we had a little back garden; when I say a little back garden, probably 30 ft long by 10–15 ft wide. It wasn't a lawn, I can tell you that, it was vegetables there for my old man; nobody had lawns, that was valuable, you couldn't eat grass but you could eat ... and I had a pet rabbit at the bottom where we used to feed them all the greens. But when they pulled the houses down I went down there one day and it was dead and ripped to pieces where the rats came out of Mill Street, because it was pretty rat infested. The old bridge which we always called Swan Bridge (Princes Bridge), the hours we spent on there, especially when the sun was going down and you could hear 'plop' – it was the water fowls, which is a water rat, you could see them plop in the water and swim across. We used to try and hit them with anything. There was hundreds of them, every house had mouse traps and stuff like that, didn't they, every one of us.

I can't really think how people managed, we're so used to having fridges.

Well, you never ever bought more than you would need really; we had a pint of milk and it was put in a cold bowl of water to try and keep it cool. I think us boys, apart from porridge, we didn't really drink much milk, perhaps as they gave it to us at school.

What shops were still down there when you were there?

You used to have Sophie Popes – right on the corner of Holloway Road and Pound Lane – a really, really old woman, she's probably the oldest woman I know or knew then; if you asked me her age then I would have said she was probably 200 years old, but at least 80; she sold everything from a nail to tea, Oxo, that type of thing. I wouldn't say she sold chocolate though, that was more Mortimore's. There was a bakery over Fordington Cross; because we used to go round Cliff, then back, I don't think my father ever saw the crust of bread for years because we used to go round and get it whilst it was hot and moan and moan until my mother cut it off; it was no cut bread of course.

There was also Forrester's in High Street Fordington.

Yes, we didn't go in there very much, or my mother didn't, we didn't really go in Sophie Pope's, it was either Mortimore's once a week, might go in twice a week up the town. We never bought vegetables and that's because my father had two allotments, one up Max Gate and one down St George's Road, so we grew everything ourselves and we used to pickle everything and put it in jars, salt things down, cabbage especially. The end of the harvest, you sat down, probably end of September like, and you had all your shallots and you sat round for a whole night, peeling and putting them in jars with those little black balls, I never knew what they did but they always put them little preservative black balls. We weren't allowed to touch those pickled onions until Christmas – which is better than what you can buy, I can tell you.

So where did you play with your mates? Was Fordington Fields or Kings Road open then?

Kings Road playing fields, they started filling that in in the early 50s (before that it had just been swamp). It used to be a water meadow and the water was, I would say, probably at deepest only about 2 ft. We used to bend the reeds down and make little walkways through there. I can remember when they built the shelter, and the day when the steam roller was delivered.

    You said other shops, well it wasn't a shop but it was a factory – the sweet factory. They used to make boiled sweets. If they smashed a jar, they couldn't sell it because it had glass and that; we used to hook the sweets out, make sure there was no glass on them.

Those poor girls in the summer, they were so hot in there and there were wasps everywhere. I remember coming outside and having a fag and just sweating because they were boiling up sugar all day, all the time.

Well, that sugar used to bring those wasps from miles around. And that galvanised fence, probably 6 ft high.

Dorchester was like an island in those days, the meadows being flooded all the way round. When it froze we would get our dads' walking sticks and a piece of slate and play ice hockey.

List of Residents in 1950

HOLLOWAY ROAD

3 – Barrett, Alfred
4 – Mintern, George
Union Arms – Rimmer, Sydney F.
10 – Whitty, Mabel Flora
11 – Lock, John
12 – Cornick, George
13 – Bascombe, Amy
14 – Northover, George
17 – McAlister, George H.
18 – Pope, Emily
19 – Baskett, Charles H.
20 – Hearn, Annie J.
32 – Burden, Leo A.C.
33 – Brown, William R.
34 – Baily, Frederick
35 – Damon, Harold R.
37 – Harrison, Henry G.
38 – Mintern, Reginald
39 – Clark, William C.
40 – Voss, Francis G.
41 – Lake, Nora E.
46 – Turnbull, Ernest
46a – Gerrard, Lorna A.
47 – Merton, Stephen F.
48 – Roberts, Elizabeth
48a – Cowdell, John T.
55 – McEwan, Robert J.
56 – White, William
57 – Damon, Constance
58 – Damon, Alfred George
59 – Holden, Emily
60 – Rollins, Ernest
61 – Brown, Arthur
62 – Lock, Albert R.C.

KINGS ROAD

4 – Allen, Emily
6 – Wright, Frederick
8 – Oates, Edward
10 – Watson, Fred
16 – Spurles, Frederick James
18 – Brewer, Joseph
20 – Smith, Marjorie P.
22 – Hallett, Ernest A.
24 – Pashen, Reuben David
26 – Legg, Ambrose T.
28 – Toms, Ernest
30 – White, Ellen
32 – Sibley, Henry
34 – Loader, Walter
36 – Clench, Charles
38 – Toms, Alfred J.
Swan Inn – Leach, Charles J.

MILL HOUSE

1 – Thorne, William Harold
2 – Rogers, Geoffrey Richard

OLD MILL FLATS

1 – Phillips, Raymond Clifford
2 – Coombes, Edward
3 – Poyter, Arthur G.
4 – Walker, Lilian
5 – Fry, Edgar Allen
6 – Charles, Robert H.
7 – Cornick, Henry R.

8 – Walker, Frederick
9 – Fry, Albert Edward

22 – White, Cecil
23 – Steed, Evelyn

HARVEY TERRACE

8 – Rose, George W.
9 – Lucas, Walter G.
10 – Baily, William
11 – Mowlem, Walter R.G.
12 – Sargent, Montague J.G.
13 – Jones, Reginald F.
14 – Lyde, Elizabeth
15 – Male, George J.
16 – Baskett, Charles H.
17 – Evans, John
18 – Lucas, Alfred J.
19 – Hawkins, Charlotte E.
20 – Vincent, Arthur W.
21 – Clarke, George

POUND LANE

1 – McKenny, Ada
2 – Tooley, Blanche Beatrice
3 – Foxwell, William Alfred
4 – Strange, Alan
6 – Hunt, Hilda
7 – Riggs, Arthur
12 – Howe, Wallace J.

STONE HOUSE

1 – Wright, Austin F.T.
2 – Loader, Reginald Herbert

Enjoying a picnic. Note the Codd-neck drinks bottles (made of clay with a marble on top).

Author's Note

In recent years, in my seventies, an interest in history led me to write my first book – *Fordington Remembered: Growing up in and Around Dorchester*. This was published by Roving Press, whose help was invaluable. Encouraged by its success, I embarked on a new adventure, writing this book about Mill Street. This proved much more difficult, due to the amount of research required. To this end, I received much-needed help from the Mill Street Memories Group, which was set up to record the memories of those who lived in or near Mill Street. Working with this dedicated group was a real pleasure, and attending the meetings was a joy – plenty of laughs and always a very pleasant atmosphere. I am grateful for their help.

I have found writing up these stories a most sad and moving experience. To think that I lived only a few hundred yards away from where all this was happening. I had no idea that this was going on, virtually under our noses. I hope this has opened your eyes and it hasn't left you with too many questions unanswered. I recently visited Mill Street with my wife Ros on a lovely afternoon – it is now a clean, quiet and attractive area to live, within easy walking distance of the town. If only my Fordington heroes Alfred Edwards and Henry Moule could see it now they would see their efforts were all worthwhile.

The Mill Street Memories Project

In early 2014 a meeting was held in the community room at Fordington Hill House, home to tenants of the Mill Street Housing Society, to find out if there was enough enthusiasm to start a project to collect memories and stories and explore the local history of the area.

Word spread and enthusiasm for the project grew beyond anyone's expectations. Packed meetings have been held in St George's Church Hall, Fordington, which have attracted over 50 people each time. Everyone enjoyed seeing the photograph collection, and forgotten memories of the life and times have surfaced quite spontaneously. Many have met old acquaintances from decades before, sometimes not since their shared childhood.

The Mill Street Memories Project objectives were to:

- collect stories, to be stored at the Dorset History Centre as well as being recorded in a book;
- provide an information board and a map of the old street layout of Mill Street;
- remove and restore the coloured glass window from the old Mission Hall;
- develop a website and upload the photo collection and stories;
- organise an exhibition;
- plot a town trail.

A small Heritage Lottery grant was successfully applied for. Donations were also given by the Mill Street Housing Society, Symonds & Sampson, and John Stark & Crickmay Partnership.

For more information see http://www.millstreethousingsociety.co.uk/.

The Mission Scouts troop, which took over from the Boys Life Brigade.

The idea of the Men's Club was to keep the men out of the pub, drinking tea, by providing games, a gramophone, sandwiches, etc.

Parading past the Methodist Chapel (left) on Kings Road at the bottom of Fordington Hill.

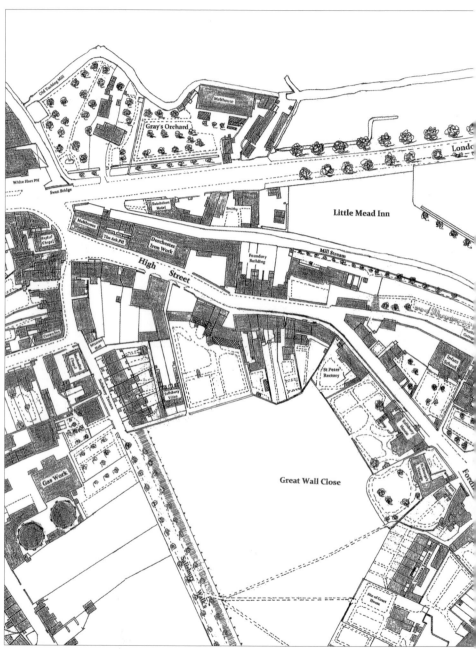

Mill Street and surrounding area c 1840. (Courtesy of Alfie Otton.)

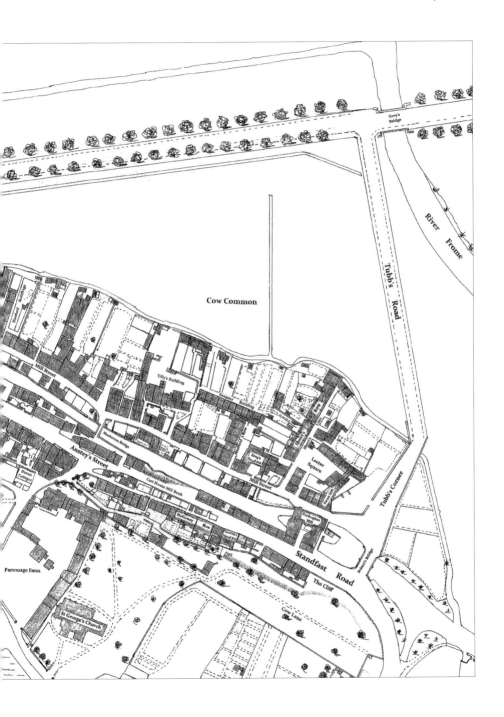

Other Books by Roving Press

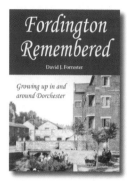

Fordington Remembered: Growing up in and around Dorchester *by David J. Forrester*

'The life of boys in a not-very advantaged part of Dorchester is vividly described, with imagery, wonder and compassion.' Terry Hearing

David Forrester's mother ran Forrester's Stores, which welcomed customers in Fordington High Street for 35 years after the Second World War. He recalls the life and times of the people going about their daily lives, through stories of growing up in the area.

His reminiscences are a record of what it was like living in post-war Fordington, including school life at St George's Infant School, Colliton Street School for Boys, and Dorchester Secondary Modern, the hey-day of Lott and Walne, market days and the old shops in Dorchester, singing in the choir, and school-boy pranks. The book is part memoir, part recollections of what life was like in an area of Dorchester known then as the 'wrong end of town'.

With author proceeds to the Rotary Foundation and Dorset ME Support Group.

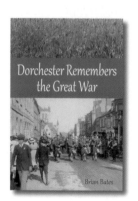

Dorchester Remembers the Great War
by Brian Bates

During the Great War of 1914–18 over 1100 men enlisted from the small market town of Dorchester. They served in such diverse theatres of war as France, India, Mesopotamia and Russia. Most of them survived that terrible conflict and returned home to tell their own unique stories. Those who did not are commemorated on the Borough's war memorials and in its two cemeteries.

This book gives a voice to those men and one woman who did not return. Through their poignant personal stories, the effect the war had on each individual and their families is revealed. But more than this, their stories weave together into a fascinating social history that shines light on the impact the war had on the very fabric of Edwardian Dorchester. The town once had the largest prisoner-of-war camp in Britain and an important military presence, yet signs of this have all but disappeared. This book brings it all to life, with an endearing look at the community of Dorchester through the Great War years.

With author proceeds to the charities Sense and Sightsavers.

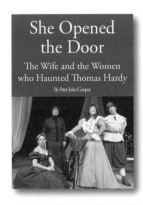

She Opened the Door
The Wife and the Women who Haunted Thomas Hardy
By Peter John Cooper

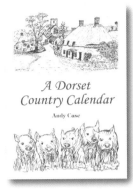

A Dorset Country Calendar
Andy Case

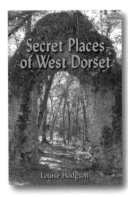

Secret Places of West Dorset
Louise Hodgson

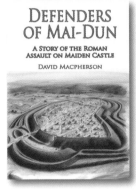

DEFENDERS OF MAI-DUN
A STORY OF THE ROMAN ASSAULT ON MAIDEN CASTLE
DAVID MACPHERSON

Discover Old Swanage
David Haysom

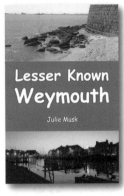

Lesser Known Weymouth
Julie Musk

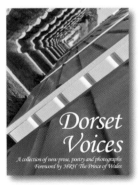

Dorset Voices
A collection of new prose, poetry and photographs
Foreword by HRH The Prince of Wales

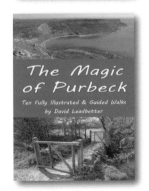

The Magic of Purbeck
Ten Fully Illustrated & Guided Walks by David Leadbetter

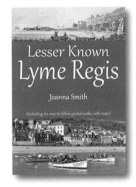

Lesser Known Lyme Regis
Joanna Smith
(Including six easy-to-follow guided walks, with maps)

Roving Press

If you like exploring Dorset, you'll love our books
www.rovingpress.co.uk, tel 01300 321531